Love on the Hot Seat

Marriage Rewind

Sherita Mitchell

Sherita Mitchell
Love on the Hot Seat

All rights reserved.
Copyright © 2024 by Sherita Mitchell

No part of this publication may be reproduced, distributed, or transmitted in any form or by any means, including photocopying, recording, or other electronic or mechanical methods, without the prior written permission of the publisher, except in the case of brief quotations embodied in critical reviews and certain other noncommercial uses permitted by copyright law.

Published by Spines
ISBN: 979-8-89569-139-7

Contents

Foreword

Marriage is a journey that many embark upon with dreams of everlasting love and companionship. However, the path to a fulfilling and enduring marriage is often fraught with challenges and obstacles that can test the very foundation of the relationship. In "Marriage Rewind," Sherita Mitchell shares her personal journey of love, loss, and redemption, offering invaluable insights and practical advice to couples who are struggling to find their way back to each other.

Through her own experiences and the lessons she has learned, Sherita provides a roadmap for couples who are facing storms of marital discord. She addresses the common issues that many relationships encounter, such as communication breakdowns, unresolved conflicts, and the damaging effects of pride and ego. With honesty and compassion, she offers strategies for healing, forgiveness, and rebuilding trust.

"Marriage Rewind" is not just a book about saving marriages; it is a testament to the power of love, commitment, and resilience. It reminds us that even in the darkest moments, there is always hope for reconciliation and renewal. Sherita's wisdom and guidance will inspire couples to fight for their relationships, to embrace vulnerability, and to commit to the work necessary to achieve a lasting and loving partnership.

Whether you are newlyweds or have been married for decades, this book will provide you with the tools and encouragement you need to strengthen your bond and create a marriage that can withstand the test of time. I encourage you to read "Marriage Rewind" with an open heart and mind and to apply the principles and practices shared within its pages.

May this book be a source of inspiration and hope for you and your spouse as you navigate the complexities of marriage and strive to build a future filled with love, joy, and mutual respect.

With warm regards,
Adam Mitchell

Chapter 1

Love on the Hot Seat –
Marriage Rewind

Marriage, often described as a journey, one that is full of joy and fulfillment but also fraught with challenges and hardships. For many couples, the path is not always smooth, and the love that once brought two people together can feel like it is slipping away. "Love on the Hot Seat: Marriage Rewind" is about those moments when your relationship feels like it has been tested by fire—when the trials and tribulations seem insurmountable and hope for reconciliation feels out of reach.

In any marriage, hurt and pain are inevitable. We hurt each other, sometimes intentionally, sometimes by accident. Words spoken in anger, actions taken in frustration, and over time, these wounds can fester, creating deep scars that seem impossible to heal. It is easy to reach a point where you want to give up, where the weight of past mistakes and the burden of unspoken grievances become too heavy to bear. But if there is one thing this book is here to remind you of it is that hope is not lost. Even when it feels like all is lost, there is still a way forward—a pathway to healing, love, and forgiveness.

Finding the Pathway to Reconciliation

Reconciliation does not happen overnight, and it does not happen without effort. It requires both parties to be willing to put in the work, to dig deep beneath the layers of pain and disappointment, and to commit to rebuilding what has been broken. This journey begins with recognizing not only the faults in your partner but also the errors you have made yourself. It is about taking responsibility for your actions and words and understanding how they have contributed to the current state of your marriage.

When you are in the middle of a crisis, it can be difficult to see beyond the hurt and the negative emotions that dominate every interaction. But it is important to remember that feelings are fleeting. They can be powerful, but they are also unreliable. What you feel in the heat of the moment may not reflect the reality of your relationship or the love that still exists beneath the surface.

This book will guide you through the process of regaining control over your emotions, learning the art of forgiveness, and letting go of the offenses that have kept you and your spouse trapped in a cycle of anger and resentment. One of the biggest obstacles to reconciliation is pride—the insistence on being right, on holding onto the principle of the matter. But sometimes, for the sake of peace and healing, we must let go of our need to win every battle. Not every disagreement needs to be a fight, and not every issue needs resolving immediately. It is about choosing your battles wisely and understanding that sometimes, letting go is the best course of action.

Respect and Loyalty: The Pillars of a Healthy Marriage

Love may be what brings two people together, but it is respect and loyalty that keep a marriage strong. Love, as beautiful and powerful as it is, can sometimes be fleeting. It can wane in the face of challenges, and if it is the only thing holding your marriage together, the foundation may not be as solid as you think. Respect, on the other hand, is something that can be relied upon. It is the acknowledgment of your partner's worth, the understanding of their value, and the commitment to treating them with dignity, even in tough times.

Loyalty goes hand in hand with respect. It is the unwavering commitment to stand by your spouse, to support them, and to work through challenges together. It is about being faithful not just in action, but in thought and intention. When respect and loyalty are at the core of your relationship, they provide a stability that love alone cannot.

Establishing Boundaries for a Stronger Marriage

One of the most important aspects of maintaining a healthy marriage is setting and respecting boundaries. Boundaries are not about keeping your spouse at a distance; they are about creating a safe space where both partners feel secure and valued. Where there are no boundaries, abuse and conflict are inevitable. This book will help you and your partner discuss and establish the boundaries that will protect your marriage and allow it to thrive.

These boundaries can take many forms. They can be physical, emotional, or even social. They might involve setting limits on how you communicate with each other, deciding how much time you spend apart, or agreeing on how you manage conflicts. Whatever form they take, the key is to mutually agree and respected by both partners.

The Journey Ahead

The journey of reconciliation is not an easy one, but it is one that can lead to profound healing and renewed love. This book invites you to embark on this journey together, to come as you are—broken, uncertain, confused—and to take the steps necessary to rebuild your marriage. It will not be easy, and there will be times when you want to give up. But remember that the path to healing is worth the effort, and that the love you shared at the beginning of your journey.

Welcome to Marriage Rewind, where we help you find that place in your marriage where you and your spouse first found each other. The road ahead may be challenging, but with respect, loyalty, and a commitment to reconciliation, it is a road that can lead to a stronger, more loving marriage.

Chapter 2

Who Did You Marry and What Makes Them Valuable?

You married a soul wrapped in flesh—someone who is a mere human, not void of mistakes. This person was born into a family that loves them dearly and has experienced many life challenges, including losses, heartbreak, and severe disappointments. They may have dealt with betrayal, scandal, backstabbing, lies, persecution, self-doubt, and insecurities. They haven't fully learned how to process all their life traumas, but through these experiences, they have gained wisdom and knowledge that can be valuable to others if they choose to let their pain become someone else's gain rather than wallowing in self-pity.

This is what truly makes someone valuable—not material possessions but having gone through the fiery trials of life and emerging like pure gold. When gold is purified, it goes through a process called "refining," which involves multiple steps to remove impurities. One of these steps is called smelting, where gold is heated to over 2,150 degrees Fahrenheit (1,046 degrees Celsius) using high pressure, heat, and chemicals. Have you ever felt the flames of life? If so, you are not alone. The fiery trial was designed to purify you, just like gold, to remove impurities from your heart and to strengthen your marriage. Only the brave can survive the purifying process, which is meant to make you better and your marriage stronger. Too often, couples jump ship because they cannot manage the trials that come with being married. There is an old saying that only the strong survive.

When two people come together, they bring with them a union of diverse life experiences. These experiences, whether good, bad, or indifferent, have shaped them into the individuals they are. Imagine, then, all these different circumstances and traumas trying to coexist under one roof. The problem arises when we try to combine all these issues with someone who has their own, attempting to create a cohesive bond that, often, feels impossible. These are the challenges we face when trying to create a good marriage, believing that simply coming together will make it so. The truth is, resolving these issues is key to building a strong marriage. Of course, it will be challenging, and friction is inevitable. This is why both parties must commit to their own self-healing to create harmony in their shared life. A person can be difficult to deal with not only in marriage but also as a roommate, coworker, or in any setting that requires close interaction. "A wounded soul, who can bear?" It is rare for people to come together completely healed and free of past issues. However, when you find someone, you love, and who loves you, there must be an understanding that you are not marrying a perfect person.

Your marriage can be a platform where you both unpack together. Both parties must commit to letting go of what wounded them, forgiving, and releasing those things. It may not happen overnight, but remember, Rome was not built in a day either. The key is to work on your own self-development, not your partner's. While you both improve yourselves, patience is required. At the end of the road, you both will be proud of the results—producing much fruit, leading to a better you and a better marriage. This then becomes a marriage that is honorable because the couple has learned the value of themselves and one another. You both can now respect and appreciate each other's worth based on the purity that has been produced within you.

The trials you have endured make you extremely valuable. Do not allow anyone to make you feel less than by judging you based on the lack or quality of your material possessions or the tough times they've seen you walk through. Your marriage is valuable even when it does not feel like it. The challenges you have faced together have made it valuable. You discover your partner's worth and value through open and transparent communication. Sharing is caring. Share with your partner the things you have experienced. The things they share with you should always be respected and appreciated.

Create a safe, judgment-free environment where you both can share tender moments and discuss the things that have wounded you. Your partner needs to trust you with their vulnerabilities. If they cannot trust you, they will not feel comfortable discussing sensitive matters. Therefore, you must be a person of integrity and build a history of being trustworthy so your partner can open up to you comfortably. This means you cannot share their personal business with family and friends just because you are upset with them. Keep your marriage private. Violating their trust in this manner could lead to them shutting down and deciding never to share anything else with you, which is harmful and unhealthy for your road to recovery and your overall relationship.

"Love on the Hot Seat: Marriage Rewind" tells your authentic story —the story of what you and your spouse have gone through separately and together. It narrates the fiery circumstances that you both had to endure to reach a higher place in your marriage, where you both can love, respect, and honor one another. Where you both had to learn to value each other's differences and lay down all the emotional and mental hindrances that blocked a better you and a successful marriage.

Once you both recognize the pitfalls and mistakes you made, and willingly and actively participate in the process of correcting them together, you have entered a place called "Marriage Rewind." Rewinding means starting over. It means letting go of what harmed you and choosing to forgive and forget. Rewinding represents forgiveness and giving each other a chance to start over again, this time armed with more wisdom and understanding—understanding your partner's worth, understanding how to treat one another, and understanding that no one is perfect. It is about appreciating the value of positive companionship, communication, respect, and honor.

Chapter 3

Knowing Your Marital Purpose

When we think about purpose, we often reflect on our individual journeys—our dreams, aspirations, and the unique contributions we wish to make in the world. However, marriage introduces a different dynamic, one that challenges us to look beyond ourselves and see the broader picture of what two people can achieve together. The concept of "marital purpose" goes far beyond the romantic ideals of love and companionship. It delves into the heart of why you and your partner were brought together and what your union is meant to accomplish.

The Power of Unity

Marriage is not just about sharing a life with someone; it is about combining strengths, balancing weaknesses, and forming a unified front. When two people are truly connected—emotionally, spiritually, and intellectually—they can create something far greater than the sum of their individual parts. This is where the concept of marital purpose comes into play. It is not just about being married; it is about understanding why you are married to this person and what you can achieve together that you could never accomplish alone.

For many couples, the idea of a marital purpose may seem abstract or even unnecessary. They might believe that the purpose of marriage is simple: to love and support one another, to raise a family, and to grow old together. While these are certainly vital aspects of marriage, there's often a deeper, more profound purpose that lies beneath the surface—one that, when discovered, can bring new meaning and direction to your relationship.

Discovering Your Marital Purpose

The journey to discovering your marital purpose begins with honest and open communication. It is important to sit down with your spouse and have a meaningful conversation about each other's strengths, weaknesses, dreams, and fears. This isn't just casual talk; it is a deep dive into understanding who you both are at your core and how those elements can work together to fulfill a greater purpose.

My husband and I had one of these conversations early in our marriage, and it was transformative. We talked about our individual talents and skills—his knack for strategic thinking, my passion for creativity—and how these could be merged to create something impactful. We prayed together, asking for guidance in aligning our individual purposes into a cohesive marital purpose. Through this process, we realized that our marriage was about more than just us; it was about what we could bring to the world together.

Once you have identified your marital purpose, the next step is to make it a priority. This purpose will become the cornerstone of your relationship, providing both of you with a shared goal that gives your marriage direction and meaning. It could be anything—a business you start together, a mission to help others, or a shared commitment to a cause you both care about deeply. Whatever it is, it should resonate with both of you and align with your shared values.

The Impact of Purpose on Marriage

Understanding and pursuing your marital purpose can be a powerful motivator, especially during tough times. Every marriage faces challenges—periods of frustration, doubt, and conflict. In these moments, it is easy to lose sight of why you are together in the first place. But when you have a clear sense of purpose, it becomes your anchor. It reminds you that your marriage is about more than just the day-to-day struggles; it is about something bigger that's worth fighting for.

A marriage without purpose is like a ship without a destination—it may float along, but it will never reach its full potential. When the passion fades and the excitement of the early day wanes, couples who lack a shared purpose may find themselves drifting apart. Without a reason to stay committed, it is easy to let the little annoyances and conflicts build up until they seem insurmountable.

But when you know your marital purpose, those same challenges take on a different light. They become obstacles to overcome together, rather than reasons to drift apart. The purpose gives you both something to fight for, a reason to stay engaged and committed, even when things get tough. It brings a sense of fulfillment that goes beyond personal satisfaction—because you are working towards something that benefits not just the two of you, but perhaps even the wider world.

Sustaining the Purpose

Finding your marital purpose is just the beginning; sustaining it requires continuous effort and intention. Life will throw distractions your way—work, children, financial pressures, and more. It is easy to get caught up in the daily grind and lose focus on your bigger goals. That's why it is important to regularly revisit your marital purpose, to ensure it remains at the forefront of your relationship.

Set aside time to talk about your progress, to celebrate your achievements, and to reassess your goals. As your marriage grows and evolves, so too might your purpose. What mattered deeply to you both in the early years may shift as you experience new phases of life together. That's okay—what's important is that you stay aligned and committed to working together towards whatever new purpose you identify.

In the end, knowing your marital purpose is about more than just having a happy marriage. It is about creating a meaningful partnership that contributes to something greater. It is about understanding that your union is not just for your own benefit, but that it has the potential to make a lasting impact—on your family, your community, and beyond. When you and your spouse are united in purpose, your marriage becomes not just a source of joy, but a powerful force for good.

And that, in the end, is the true purpose of marriage.

Chapter 4

Vow Renewal

In any marriage, there may come a time when you and your spouse feel the need for a fresh start, a moment to pause, reflect, and recommit to the journey you have embarked on together. Vow renewals offer a powerful way to reaffirm your love and dedication, marking a new chapter in your relationship. Whether you have been married for just a few years or several decades, renewing your vows can bring a refreshing and meaningful dimension to your marriage.

The Importance of Renewing Vows

Renewing your vows is much more than a ceremonial nod to the past; it is a forward-looking affirmation of your commitment to each other. It is a chance to revisit the promises you made on your wedding day and to celebrate how far you have come as a couple. This act serves as a tangible reminder of your enduring love, a symbol that your relationship continues to grow and evolve.

In many ways, vow renewals can be a powerful way to reinforce the foundation of your marriage. They provide an opportunity to acknowledge the challenges you have faced and the ways you have grown together. It is a moment to express gratitude for your partner's presence in your life and to set your sights on the future with renewed optimism and commitment.

When to Renew Your Vows

There's no right or wrong time to renew your vows. Some couples choose to do it to mark significant milestones like a major anniversary—10, 25, or 50 years together, for example. Others may choose to renew their vows after overcoming a particularly challenging period in their marriage, using the ceremony to celebrate their resilience and the strength of their bond.

It is important to remember that the number of years you have been married does not dictate when it is time for a renewal. What matters most is your shared desire to reconnect and reaffirm your commitment. Whether you have been married for five years or fifty, if you feel the need to renew your vows, it is the right time.

Planning Your Vow Renewal

Planning a vow renewal ceremony is a deeply personal process that should reflect the unique nature of your relationship. Here are some options to consider:

Private Renewal: For some couples, the most meaningful way to renew vows is through a private, intimate ceremony. Whether it is a special getaway to a favorite destination or a quiet moment in your own home, a private renewal allows you to focus solely on each other, free from distractions. This setting can be especially powerful if you are looking to reconnect on a deeper level.

With Close Family and Friends: If you prefer to share your joy and commitment with those closest to you, consider a small ceremony with family and close friends. This option allows you to include the people who have supported you throughout your marriage, making the occasion even more meaningful. It is a beautiful way to celebrate your love with those who matter most.

Larger Celebration: Some couples choose to go all out with a larger celebration, reminiscent of a second wedding. This can be a festive event that includes extended family, friends, and even colleagues. A larger celebration can be a wonderful way to honor your marriage on a grand scale, creating lasting memories with all the people who have been part of your journey.

Elements of a Vow Renewal

To make your vow renewal ceremony truly special, consider incorporating elements that resonate with you as a couple:

Personal Vows: Writing new vows or reaffirming the original ones is one of the most significant aspects of a vow renewal. Take the time to speak from the heart, reflecting on what your spouse means to you now and your hopes for the future. This is your chance to express your love and commitment in a way that's deeply personal and meaningful.

Symbolic Gestures: Many couples choose to include symbolic gestures in their vow renewal ceremony. This could be lighting a unity candle, exchanging new rings, or even planting a tree together. These gestures add a layer of meaning to the ceremony, symbolizing the continued growth and unity of your relationship.

Meaningful Location: The location of your vow renewal can add another dimension to the experience. Consider choosing a place that holds special significance for both of you—the spot where you first met, got engaged, or shared a memorable experience. A meaningful location can evoke powerful emotions and create a lasting memory.

The Benefits of Renewing Vows

Renewing your vows offers numerous benefits that can strengthen your marriage:

Reaffirmation of Commitment: By renewing your vows, you are reinforcing the commitment you have made to each other. It is a public or private declaration that your love is still strong and that you are both dedicated to making your marriage thrive.

Strengthening the Bond: The process of preparing for and participating in a vow renewal ceremony can bring you closer together. It is an opportunity to reflect on your journey as a couple, to appreciate how far you have come, and to reaffirm the bond that holds you together.

Creating New Memories: A vow renewal is a chance to create new, joyful memories that you can look back on with fondness. These memories serve as reminders of the love and commitment you share, giving you something special to hold onto in the years to come.

Inspiration for the Future: Most importantly, renewing your vows can inspire you to continue nurturing your relationship. It serves as a reminder of the promises you have made and the future you are building together, motivating you to face whatever challenges lie ahead with renewed strength and determination.

Making it Personal

Your vow renewal should reflect your unique relationship. Whether you choose a grand celebration or a quiet, private moment, the key is that it resonates with both of you. Don't feel pressured to follow a specific formula—do what feels right for you and your marriage. The most important thing is that the ceremony is meaningful to both of you and strengthens the bond you share.

Renewing your vows is a beautiful way to celebrate your love and commitment. It is a reminder of the journey you have taken together and a promise to continue supporting and loving each other in the years to come. Do not wait for a specific milestone; if you feel the need to renew your vows, embrace it and make it a special occasion that strengthens your bond.

Chapter 5

Setting Marital Boundaries

Establishing boundaries in your relationship is crucial for fostering accountability and trust and for preventing unnecessary conflict in your marriage. Where there are no boundaries, chaos and confusion tend to prevail. But what exactly are boundaries, and why are they so important in a relationship?

Understanding Boundaries

A boundary is a line that marks the limits of an area, showing where one thing ends, and another begins. In relationships, boundaries define what each person is comfortable with and how they expect to be treated. Everyone's boundaries are different; what one person may tolerate, another may not. It is essential to know, understand, and respect each other's boundaries.

Often, people bring habits from previous relationships into their current ones without realizing that these actions might not be acceptable to their new partner. If a previous relationship was more lenient about certain things, you might instinctively do things that your current partner does not approve of. This is why it is important to dwell with one another according to knowledge and understanding.

The Purpose of Boundaries

Boundaries maintain the integrity of a relationship. Just as laws are established to keep order and peace in society, boundaries are set in relationships to protect both individuals involved. Without boundaries, people might behave in ways that are harmful or offensive to others, which is why we have rules and consequences in place, such as the prison system for those who overstep societal limits.

Similarly, boundaries in a marriage protect the relationship from harm. For example, there are natural boundaries, like those that keep the sun at a safe distance from Earth, or boundaries that keep the oceans contained to prevent flooding. Parents set boundaries for their children to protect them, such as curfews to reduce the risk of harm. Even religious laws serve as boundaries to protect the soul from sinful behavior.

Given these examples, it is fitting that we establish boundaries in our relationships and marriages to protect and maintain their integrity. Boundaries are not one-size fits-all; they should be mutually agreed upon and tailored to what both partners consider acceptable or unacceptable.

Discussing and Establishing Boundaries

It is essential to discuss boundaries early on in a relationship. For instance, some couples may not mind if their spouse goes out with friends of the opposite sex, while others might be uncomfortable with this. Similarly, one partner may not like it if the other stays out all night with friends. If such behavior is unacceptable in your relationship, it should be discussed maturely and respectfully, and a boundary should be set.

Examples of Crossing Boundaries

1. Inappropriate relationships
2. Inappropriate conversations and flirting
3. Disrespectful behavior and communication
4. Betrayal of any kind
5. Physical, verbal, or emotional abuse
6. Lying
7. Gossiping about your spouse to others
8. Stealing from your spouse
9. Withholding important information or hiding money
10. Being dishonest about your past
11. Keeping secrets

The Importance of Healthy Boundaries

Establishing healthy boundaries in your marriage not only protects the relationship but also protects you as an individual. Just like there are consequences for breaking natural and spiritual laws, there are unforeseen consequences for breaking the boundaries or covenants you and your spouse have set. These consequences could lead to the breakdown of your relationship, a broken family, or even financial devastation.

Remember, for every action, there is a reaction. One bad decision can have a significant impact on your life and marriage. Be mindful of the decisions you make and the boundaries that have been set. By doing so, you can maintain peace, strengthen accountability, and build a strong bond of trust in your marriage that will be exemplary for others, including your children.

Chapter 6

Identifying the Enemies of Your Marriage

Marriage is a beautiful and complex journey that requires effort, dedication, and awareness. One of the most crucial aspects of maintaining a strong marriage is the ability to recognize and address the external threats that can slowly erode your relationship. It is a sad reality that not everyone in your life wants to see you happy or in a successful partnership. These "marriage breakers" can be subtle, often hidden behind the guise of concern or friendship, making them difficult to detect. They can come from various sources, including jealous family members, co-workers, or even friends you once trusted.

Understanding and identifying these threats early on can make all the difference in keeping your marriage strong and intact. Let's explore some of the signs that someone in your life may be an enemy to your marriage and how you can protect your relationship from these harmful influences.

Signs of Marriage Enemies

Always Speaking Negatively About Your Spouse: Pay close attention to anyone who consistently speaks poorly of your spouse. Their negative comments, no matter how subtle, can sow seeds of doubt and resentment in your mind. Over time, these seeds can grow into major issues that may threaten the stability of your relationship.

Encourages Divorce: Be wary of individuals who suggest divorce as the first solution to any marital problem you share with them. Instead of offering support or advice on how to work through issues, these people may push you towards separation, reflecting their own biases or unhappiness.

Excludes Your Spouse: If someone in your life frequently invites you to events or gatherings where your spouse isn't welcomed, this exclusion can create a sense of division and insecurity. It is a subtle but effective way to drive a wedge between you and your partner.

Social Media Behavior: In today's digital age, even something as simple as social media behavior can be telling. Notice if someone never likes or acknowledges pictures of you and your spouse together. This seemingly trivial act can indicate underlying jealousy or disapproval of your relationship.

Fake Smiles: Trust your instincts. If you sense that someone's smiles and friendly gestures are insincere or disingenuous when it comes to your marriage, it is important to take note. These individuals may not have your best interests at heart.

Gossiping: Gossip is a toxic behavior, especially when it involves your spouse. Be cautious of those who spread rumors or gossip about your partner. This behavior is harmful and can create unnecessary conflict and tension between you and your spouse.

Fault Finding: Some people seem to take pleasure in finding faults in others. If someone in your life constantly points out flaws in your spouse or your relationship, they may have a hidden agenda. Their goal could be to undermine your marriage by highlighting perceived shortcomings.

Bringing Up the Past: Beware of individuals who continually bring up past mistakes or issues in your relationship. By doing so, they prevent you from moving forward and healing. They may have their own reasons for wanting to keep old wounds open.

Matchmaking Attempts: It is a red flag if someone in your life is trying to hook you up with other people, especially if they know you are married. This clear undermining of your marriage shows a lack of respect for your relationship.

Inappropriate Behavior: Pay attention to those who exhibit inappropriate behavior around your significant other, especially when you are not around. This can include making suggestive comments or acting in ways that cross boundaries. Such behavior is disrespectful and can create tension between you and your spouse.

Single Friends' Influence: While it is important to maintain friendships outside of your marriage, be cautious if single friends frequently encourage you to spend time with them in ways that do not align with your marital commitments. Their influence can subtly promote a lifestyle that conflicts with the values of your marriage.

Disgruntled In-Laws: Family dynamics can be challenging, especially when in-laws are openly negative or hostile towards your spouse. Address these issues directly, as unresolved tension with in-laws can create significant rifts in your marriage.

Too Much Time Apart: Spending excessive time apart, whether due to work, social commitments, or other reasons, can weaken the bond between you and your spouse. It can also create opportunities for misunderstandings, temptations, and the intrusion of negative influences.

Protecting Your Marriage

Recognizing the potential enemies of your marriage is only half the battle. The next step is to actively protect your relationship from these threats. Here are some strategies to help you and your spouse safeguard your marriage:

Open Communication:One of the most effective ways to protect your marriage is through open and honest communication. Discuss any concerns you have with your spouse and listen to their perspective as well. Transparency is key to identifying and addressing external threats together.

Set Boundaries:Establish clear boundaries with friends, family, and co-workers. Let it be known that negative talk about your spouse or relationship is unacceptable. These boundaries create a protective barrier around your marriage, deterring those who might otherwise bring harm.

Stay United:Present a united front in both public and private settings. This solidarity not only strengthens your relationship but also sends a clear message to others that your marriage is strong and not easily shaken.

Prioritize Your Relationship:Make your marriage a priority by spending quality time together and ensuring that you are meeting each other's emotional and physical needs. A strong, connected relationship is less vulnerable to external threats.

Seek Positive Influences:Surround yourselves with people who support and respect your marriage. Positive influences, whether they be friends, family, or mentors, can provide encouragement and reinforce your commitment to each other.

Address Issues Promptly:If you identify a potential threat to your marriage, address it promptly and constructively. Delaying action can allow the issue to fester and grow, potentially causing more harm than dealt with early on.

Encourage Positive Relationships:Foster and encourage positive relationships with family and friends who respect your marriage. Encourage your spouse to build bonds with these supportive individuals, as they can be a valuable source of strength and encouragement.

Identifying and addressing the enemies of your marriage is crucial for maintaining a strong and healthy relationship. By staying vigilant and initiative-taking, you can protect your marriage from negative influences and ensure that your bond remains resilient. Remember, the strength of your marriage is not just about the love you share but also about the efforts you make to guard that love against the challenges and threats that come your way.

Discuss these signs with your spouse and work together to create a supportive and loving environment where your marriage can thrive. Your relationship deserves every effort to keep it strong, happy, and protected from those who may wish to see it falter.

Chapter 7

When the In-Laws Become the Outlaws

The Challenges of In-Laws

What can I say about this? Getting married comes with the added dynamic of your spouse's family. Some people are fortunate enough to marry into a family where the in-laws are warm, welcoming, and easy to have a good relationship with. However, others are not so lucky and find themselves dealing with in-laws who are not as pleasant. If you struggle to have a good relationship with some of your spouse's family members, know that you are not alone. It is a common experience, and the reasons behind it can vary widely. Some people may never accept you, no matter who you are or what you do to be accepted. The best approach is to offer your love and kindness, be yourself, and never let anyone make you feel uncomfortable in their presence.

Managing Uncomfortable Situations

It can be incredibly uncomfortable when you and your spouse attend a family function, and one or more family members clearly do not like you. What should you do in such a situation? The answer might surprise you: do nothing. It is important to remember that you are married to one person, and that person is your spouse. If a member of their family does not like you, that is their issue, especially if you have done nothing to provoke this ill will against you. Their feelings are not your responsibility, and you should not allow their negativity to impact your well-being.

The Impact of Sharing Marital Issues

Sometimes, the root of the problem lies in what your spouse may have shared with their family during a rough patch in your relationship. Family members can hold onto these grievances long after you and your spouse have reconciled. This is why it is so crucial to keep your marital business private. Sharing too much with family can create lasting tensions that may be difficult to resolve. When you find yourself dealing with in-laws who hold a grudge or have an attitude problem, the best course of action is often to ignore them and not let their negativity affect you.

Attending Family Functions

Some people choose to avoid family functions altogether to steer clear of troublesome in-laws. I completely disagree with this approach. Avoiding family events means that your spouse will likely attend without you, which isn't fair to them. It can lead to frustration and resentment in a spouse who genuinely wants you by their side. Avoidance isn't a healthy way to deal with the situation, especially when you are trying to strengthen your relationship.

A United Front

You and your spouse should attend these events together, supporting each other and presenting a strong, united front. Never let someone intimidate you to the point where you feel the need to stay away. You don't have to engage with troublesome individuals. While you are there, smile, have an enjoyable time, and bring your positive energy. Do not let anyone change who you are or shift your mood to accommodate their misery. Love and positivity are infectious, so spread as much as you can.

Managing Negative In-Laws

If they choose to behave poorly, let them. You should remain unbothered and refuse to participate in their negativity. To really throw them off, greet them with a smile and keep moving. They will not know how to react to your kindness in the face of their meanness. Keep being yourself! You and your spouse have worked hard to build and heal your relationship, and you should not let anyone disrupt what you have achieved together.

Moving Forward

It is often said, it is the little foxes that spoil the vine, so keep moving forward in your marriage rewind journey. By standing united and supporting each other, you can navigate the challenges posed by difficult in-laws. Remember, your marriage is about the two of you, and maintaining your bond is the priority.

Dealing with difficult in-laws can be a challenge, but it is essential to handle these situations with grace and positivity. By staying true to yourself and supporting your spouse, you can rise above the negativity and continue building a strong, healthy relationship. Stay united, stay positive, and keep moving forward in your marriage rewind journey.

Chapter 8

Familiarity Breeds Contempt

Understanding Familiarity and Contempt

As married couples, we naturally become familiar with our spouses over time. We know their habits, quirks, and routines, and this deep familiarity is a hallmark of a close relationship. However, the saying "familiarity breeds contempt" underscores a potential pitfall: the more time we spend with someone, the more likely we are to feel comfortable saying or doing things that might be disrespectful, often without realizing the harm we are causing. This can lead to taking your spouse for granted, which can erode the respect and admiration that once formed the foundation of your relationship.

Maintaining Respect

It is crucial to avoid losing sight of the amazing person you married. Even as you grow more familiar with your spouse, continue to see them with the same positive regard you had when you first met. This is not just about keeping the spark alive; it is about maintaining the respect that is essential for a healthy relationship. Teach your children to respect both you and your spouse by modeling it in your daily interactions. While it is important to keep your relationship light and playful, setting boundaries on how you speak to and treat each other is necessary to prevent familiarity from turning into contempt.

The Dangers of Unchecked Familiarity

Unchecked familiarity can lead to a slow but steady decline in the quality of your relationship. Disrespect, even in small doses, can accumulate and cause significant harm over time. This principle applies not only to marriages but to all relationships, including friendships and professional partnerships. It is important to consistently remind yourself of the reasons you married your spouse and to nurture the respect and love you had when you first began your journey together. Doing so can prevent the negative effects of familiarity from creeping in.

Strategies to Maintain Respect

- Regular Appreciation:Continuously show appreciation for your spouse. Recognize the small and important things they do and express your gratitude often. This keeps the relationship grounded in positivity and mutual respect.
- Set Boundaries:Establish clear boundaries about what is acceptable behavior and language in your relationship. Make sure both partners understand and respect these boundaries to prevent disrespect from becoming a habit.
- Positive Communication:Communicate in a positive and constructive manner. Avoid negative comments, sarcasm, and harsh criticism. Instead, focus on uplifting and encouraging each other, which strengthens the bond between you.

- Quality Time:Spend quality time together, away from distractions. Engage in activities that you both enjoy, which can help you reconnect and reinforce your relationship.
- Respectful Disagreements:When disagreements arise, handle them with respect. Avoid name-calling, shouting, or bringing up past issues that have already been resolved. Approach conflicts with a mindset of resolution, not blame.
- Lead by Example:If you have children, model respectful behavior. Show them how to treat their future partners by demonstrating respect and love in your own relationship.
- Continual Growth:Keep growing together. Attend workshops, read books, or engage in activities that promote relationship growth and understanding. Continuous learning and improvement can help keep your relationship strong and resilient.

Familiarity in marriage can easily lead to contempt if not carefully managed. By continuously appreciating, respecting, and positively communicating with your spouse, you can maintain a healthy and loving relationship. Setting and upholding boundaries, spending quality time together, and modeling respectful behavior for your children are all crucial steps in preserving the respect and admiration you had for each other when you first met. Remember, maintaining respect and love in your marriage is an ongoing journey that requires effort and commitment from both partners.

Chapter 9

Choose Your Battles Wisely

Not All Concerns Need to Be Addressed

When working to heal and strengthen your relationship, it is essential to understand that not every issue needs to be addressed. Sometimes, constant bickering can do more harm than good. Choosing your battles wisely means discerning which issues are important and which ones can be let go. It is about knowing when to speak up and when to allow things to pass without conflict.

Playing Games is a No, No!

As adults, we know that playing mental and emotional games with each other is unhealthy, yet it is a behavior many couples still engage in. These games only serve to degrade the relationship further and create more problems. When you play games with your spouse, you introduce a toxic element into the marriage that can cause lasting damage.

The Dangers of Playing Games

1. **Jealousy Games:**One of the most common games couples play involves trying to make their spouse jealous by pretending to be interested in someone else. This behavior is incredibly dangerous. If your partner believes you are engaging with someone else romantically, it might prompt them to do the same, leading to a spiral of mistrust and hurt.
2. **Love Games:**Another harmful game is making your partner believe you don't love them. Couples might do this by saying or doing things that suggest they've fallen out of love. This is often an emotional defense mechanism used to gain power in the relationship, but it only causes more harm and creates emotional distance.

Removing Games from Your Relationship

To build a strong, healthy marriage, all game-playing needs to be eliminated. For example, a common scenario might be dressing up and looking your best just to leave the house to make your partner jealous and see if they still care. While it might seem harmless, these games are destructive and only serve to undermine trust and connection in the relationship.

Letting Go of Individual Pain

When two people come together in a marriage, they can help each other grow and evolve. Often, our spouses can see our character flaws more clearly than we can. While others might notice these flaws and talk about them behind our backs, a spouse is more likely to confront us directly. However, when this feedback is delivered harshly, it can be difficult to receive.

Accepting Constructive Criticism

Even if the delivery of the feedback is not pleasant, it is important to consider whether there's truth in what's being said. My father used to say, "Everyone is not wrong about you." If multiple people are pointing out the same behavior, it is likely that there is some validity to their observations. Instead of reacting with anger or defensiveness, take the time to reflect and engage in self-examination. If their feedback holds truth, work on improving yourself.

Letting Go of Past Hurts

It is common to react to situations based on past hurt, pain, and disappointments. However, carrying these unresolved issues into your current relationship is unfair to your partner and can prevent your marriage from thriving. To have a healthy relationship, you must learn to let go of the things that keep you stuck in the past.

Steps to Letting Go

1. **Self-Examination:** Start by examining yourself and recognizing the validity of any feedback you have received about your behavior.
2. **Seek Help:** If needed, seek professional help to work through past issues that may be holding you back.

3. **Forgiveness:**Practice forgiveness towards those who have hurt you in the past, including yourself.
4. **Acceptance:**Accept the situation for what it was and make a conscious decision to let go of it.
5. **Move Forward:**Focus on building a healthy and loving relationship with your partner, free from the baggage of past hurts.

The Importance of Letting Go

Unresolved issues from the past can keep you in emotional chains, dragging these unresolved feelings from relationship to relationship. It is time to disconnect from your negative past so you can love your spouse wholeheartedly. Letting go to is a choice and a decision you must make for yourself. It often involves accepting the situation, forgiving, and making a conscious decision to move on.

Choosing your battles wisely and letting go of individual pain are crucial steps in healing and strengthening your marriage. By avoiding unnecessary conflicts and removing harmful games, you can create a healthier, more supportive relationship. Letting go of past hurts allows you to love your spouse without the burden of unresolved issues, leading to a more fulfilling and joyful marriage.

Chapter 10

Married but Separated

Understanding Separation Within Marriage

Every marriage will go through periods of distance, especially in long-term relationships. However, separation does not always mean living in different homes. It is entirely possible to be living under the same roof as your spouse yet feel miles apart emotionally and physically. I've seen this happen, and I've even experienced it myself in a previous relationship before I married my current husband. We reached a point where we just could not get along, and I decided to sleep in a separate bedroom.

Can You Hear Me Now?

Understanding the Signals

When your partner decides to retreat to a separate bedroom, it is a clear sign that something is deeply wrong. This action often signals that they feel there's no way to resolve the ongoing issues, and they're exhausted from trying. Moving into a separate space is not just about needing physical distance; it is a loud and clear demonstration of their frustrations and aggravations. It is their way of trying to get you to listen —to really hear them and understand the unresolved issues that are straining the relationship.

The Significance of Sleeping in Separate Bedrooms

When a couple begins sleeping in separate bedrooms, it is a clear signal that there are unresolved issues at play. This behavior is more than just a temporary measure; it is often a manifestation of deeper problems within the relationship. If left unchecked, this kind of separation can lead to a more permanent rift or further exacerbate existing conflicts. Before a couple ever separates physically in the bedroom, there has already been a separation in the heart and mind. Unresolved matters create emotional distance, which can eventually manifest in physical distance.

The Importance of Addressing Issues Early

This is why it is so critical to address issues as soon as they arise. The longer problems left unspoken and unresolved, the wider the gap between you and your spouse will become. Open communication is key to understanding each other's perspectives and working towards resolutions that both partners can agree on. Ignoring issues does not make them disappear; it only allows them to fester and grow, leading to greater emotional and physical separation.

Preventing Emotional and Physical Separation

Maintaining a strong bond requires constant effort and a commitment to communication. It is important to talk through your disagreements, understand the root causes of your conflicts, and work together to find solutions. By doing so, you can prevent the emotional and physical separation that can otherwise turn a marriage into a relationship of convenience rather than a partnership built on love and mutual respect.

Living together but feeling separated is a painful experience that many couples go through, but it does not have to be the end of the relationship. By addressing issues early, keeping communication lines open, and working actively to resolve conflicts, you can overcome these challenges and restore the connection that brought you together in the first place. Your marriage is worth fighting for, and with effort and understanding, you can bridge the gap that may have formed and find your way back to each other.

Chapter 11

Power Struggles

Understanding Power Struggles

Power struggles are a significant issue in many marriages and deserve careful attention. A "power struggle" happens when two or more people compete for control or authority. When this becomes a pattern in a marriage, it is a clear sign that something is off balance. It usually indicates that one or both partners do not fully understand or respect their roles within the relationship, which can lead to conflict and discord.

ROLES

Understanding Traditional Roles in Marriage

Traditionally, the husband has been viewed as the head of the household, while the wife has often taken on a supportive role. This dynamic, rooted in cultural and historical contexts, was to create a balance within the home, where each partner had distinct responsibilities that contributed to the family's overall well-being.

However, it is crucial to recognize that these roles are not about dominance or control. The true purpose of these roles is to foster harmony and cooperation within the marriage. When both partners understand and embrace their roles with mutual respect and a shared commitment to each other's well-being, the relationship can thrive.

Avoiding Misunderstandings and Misuses of Traditional Roles

Misunderstanding the purpose of traditional roles can lead to abuse or resentment. If one partner views their role as a means of exerting control or power over the other, it can create a toxic dynamic that undermines the foundation of the marriage. Similarly, if a partner feels forced into a role, they are uncomfortable with, it can lead to feelings of frustration, resentment, and disconnection.

To avoid these pitfalls, it is important for couples to communicate openly about their expectations and desires regarding their roles within the marriage. Both partners should feel empowered to express their needs and preferences and to negotiate responsibilities in a way that feels fair and equitable to both.

Mutual Agreement and Flexibility

Responsibilities and roles in a marriage should be mutually agreed upon. This means that both partners should have a say in how tasks are divided and should feel comfortable with the roles they take on. It is also important to recognize that roles can evolve over time. What works for a couple at one stage of their life may need to be adjusted as circumstances change, such as when children are born, careers change, or personal interests develop.

Flexibility is key to maintaining a healthy balance in a marriage. Partners should be willing to reassess their roles periodically and adjust as needed. This not only helps to prevent resentment but also ensures that both partners feel valued and supported in their relationship.

Building a Partnership Based on Respect and Cooperation

Ultimately, a successful marriage is built on a foundation of mutual respect, understanding, and cooperation. When both partners view their roles as complementary rather than hierarchical, they can work together to create a partnership that supports each other's growth and happiness.

It is about finding a balance that works for both partners and recognizing that every couple is unique. By embracing open communication and a willingness to adapt, couples can create a harmonious and fulfilling marriage that respects both traditional values and modern sensibilities.

The Need for Control

Everyone has a natural desire to be in control; it is a basic human instinct. But in a marriage, if both partners are constantly vying for control, it can create a toxic environment. It is like having two heads on one body—neither can function properly without creating chaos. That's why it is crucial for couples to sit down and discuss who is responsible for what within the marriage. When both partners are on the same page and working toward the same goals, power struggles become unnecessary. Clearly defined roles and mutual agreement on responsibilities can prevent much of the unnecessary conflict that arises in a household.

Avoiding Power Struggles

Positive outcomes are more likely when everyone in the relationship understands and respects their roles. Power struggles often occur when someone oversteps their boundaries or takes on responsibilities that aren't theirs to begin with. Here's a little secret, especially for the ladies: you have incredible gifts and talents that can significantly contribute to your marriage and family. As a wife, your role is supportive, but that does not mean it is less important. In fact, you are the driving force behind your husband's success.

The Role of Support

The saying "behind every strong man, there's a strong woman" holds a lot of truth. Men are often designed to lead, provide, and protect, and when you allow your husband to take on that role without competing for control, you empower him to be his best self. When a husband feels supported and loved, he's more likely to thrive, and this creates a positive cycle of mutual respect and empowerment. However, this only works if the husband is fulfilling his responsibilities in caring for his wife. If a wife feels neglected or unsupported, power struggles are almost inevitable, especially if she feels she must step in to meet household needs.

Sharing Responsibilities

When a woman finds herself taking on her husband's responsibilities, she might begin to feel like she's the head of the household, especially if she's doing things that are typically his duties. This can lead to a shift in dynamics that creates tension and conflict. To avoid this, it is essential that everyone in the household understands their roles and responsibilities, including the children. When things are done decently and in order, the household can function smoothly, with everyone contributing in a way that aligns with their strengths.

Key to Success

The key to a successful marriage is understanding and respecting each other's roles. Everyone has their own unique power and capabilities. If you focus on tapping into your own strengths rather than competing for control, you'll find that the relationship functions much more smoothly. By embracing your own role and allowing your partner to do the same, you create a balanced, harmonious relationship where both partners feel valued and respected.

Maintaining harmony in your marriage means recognizing and supporting each other's strengths. By avoiding unnecessary power struggles and embracing your unique contributions, you can build a partnership that thrives on mutual respect and shared goals.

Chapter 12

Honor vs. Respect

In my book, I discussed the importance of respect in maintaining a healthy relationship. Respect is indeed crucial for any partnership, as it fosters trust, understanding, and communication between two people. However, there is another attribute that is equally important, if not more so, in a marriage—honor.

Honor is a concept that is not often talked about in the context of marriage, but it plays a vital role in creating a strong and lasting bond between partners. Honor goes beyond respect; it is the "golden key" that can unlock blessings and favor in your marriage. When honor is missing, relationships suffer. Honoring your spouse is essential for a thriving marriage, as it strengthens the foundation upon which your relationship is built.

What is Honor?

Honor represents the highest level of respect you can give to someone. To honor someone is to add great value and weight to them, treating them with special recognition and esteem. It involves placing significant importance on your partner and understanding their true worth. When you honor your spouse, you express how valuable they are in your eyes and demonstrate that value through your actions and words.

Honor is about recognizing the unique qualities and characteristics that make your spouse special. It is about understanding their strengths, appreciating their efforts, and celebrating their contributions to your life and relationship. Honor requires a deep awareness of your partner's worth, beyond superficial attributes like appearance, wealth, or material possessions. It is about valuing the person they are at their core—their kindness, compassion, reliability, and integrity.

Understanding Your Partner's Value

Many people enter marriage without a clear understanding of their partner's true value. They may focus on superficial qualities such as looks, financial status, or social standing, but these factors do not define a person's worth. True value lies in how a person treats others, their capacity for empathy and compassion, and their commitment to living a life of integrity and honor.

Valuable qualities in a person can be seen in their selflessness, kindness, and the way they care for those who are less fortunate. It is evident in their actions, decisions, and the condition of their heart. Being trustworthy, reliable, and honest makes a person valuable, not the size of their house or the price of their car. Understanding this can help couples truly honor each other and build a stronger, more meaningful relationship.

Celebrating What Makes Your Partner Great

To honor your spouse, it is important to recognize and celebrate the qualities that make them great. Whether it is their kindness, their sense of humor, their dedication to their family, or their hard work, these attributes should be acknowledged and cherished. You should be your spouse's biggest supporter, championing their achievements and standing by them through challenges. Honor them in private and public, among family and friends, and make it clear that you value and appreciate them deeply.

When you honor your spouse, you create a positive environment where respect and admiration flourish. This kind of environment breeds confidence, assurance, and affirmation, building strong bonds that are resilient to the pressures and stresses of life. By honoring each other, couples set the standard for how they expect to be treated, not just by each other but by others as well.

Honor and Protection Go Hand in Hand

Part of honoring your spouse is protecting them—physically, emotionally, and mentally. Protecting your partner goes beyond just safeguarding them from physical harm. It also involves shielding them from emotional pain and mental stress. Here are three keyways to protect your spouse:

1. Physical Protection: Ensure that your spouse is safe from all physical harm and threats. This includes being vigilant about their safety and well-being and stepping in whenever they are in danger.

2. Emotional Protection: Safeguard your spouse's emotional well-being by:

- Avoiding verbal abuse and discouraging it from others.
- Not sharing negative comments or gossip about them.
- Defending their character if attacked.
- Shielding them from unwelcome news or situations that could overwhelm them emotionally.
- Encouraging them to take time for themselves when needed.
- Being honest, faithful, and supportive, showing consistent care and empathy.

3. Mental Protection: Help maintain your spouse's mental health by:

- Minimizing stress whenever possible.
- Assisting with household responsibilities to reduce their burden.
- Encouraging healthy habits, like regular workouts and proper relaxation.
- Planning vacations and leisure activities to help them unwind.
- Avoiding unnecessary conflicts that could cause mental strain.
- Being a supportive and understanding partner, always ready to help and listen.

Protecting your partner in these ways shows that you honor and value them. It demonstrates your commitment to their well-being and reinforces the bond you share. By consistently showing honor and protection, you build a marriage based on mutual respect, love, and deep appreciation.

In every relationship, both honor and respect are essential. While respect lays the groundwork for trust and understanding, honor elevates the relationship to a place of deep connection and unwavering support. By honoring each other, couples can create a marriage that is not only strong but also filled with joy, peace, and a profound sense of fulfillment.

Chapter 13

Managing Emotions and Conflict Resolution

Uncontrolled Emotions

What are Emotions? Emotions are a conscious mental reaction to certain situations. They range from feelings of love, fear, and anger to hatred. You may have noticed that certain people or circumstances can trigger different emotions in you—some might make you act out of character, while others bring you joy. Life events like the death of a loved one, or losing a job, home, or car, can cause a flood of negative emotions. In your relationship, it is vital to learn how to control these emotions, even when provoked. Controlling your emotions is a form of self-mastery. When someone can shift your mood from happiness to anger, they have taken control of your mind, and you have given them power over you. It is time to reclaim that power and strengthen your relationship.

Uncontrolled emotions often lead us to say and do things to our spouses that we later regret. We might think it is okay to be rude or obnoxious because we're married and comfortable with each other, but that's far from the truth. The person you are committed to should be treated with the highest level of respect. How you react to each other, especially in tense moments, can determine the success of your marriage.

How Do You Control Your Emotions?

When someone presents an issue aggressively, the natural response is to defend yourself. But before you react, take a moment to breathe. Remember, you have the power to shift the emotional atmosphere in the room. Never let anyone's negative energy control your attitude. Instead, respond calmly and confidently. For example, you might say, "I'm sorry you are upset. If I did something to cause this reaction, I apologize. However, I'm not used to handling matters this way. If you'd like to talk about it, I'm happy to discuss it so we can resolve this like adults."

By responding this way, you have diffused the situation, maintained control over your emotions, and taken charge of the emotional environ ment. It is not always easy, especially if you struggle with anger, but with practice and consistency, you can master your emotions and control the atmosphere around you.

Making Decisions When Angry-The Danger of Angry Decisions

Whether in a relationship or not, making decisions while angry is unwise and immature. When emotions are high, it is the worst time to make any significant decisions. Anger clouds judgment, and decisions made in anger often lead to regret.

Examples of Rash Decisions

In the heat of an argument, people often make impulsive decisions that can complicate matters further. Here are some common examples:

Moving Out: Packing up and leaving the house, only to regret it and must move back in later.

Filing for Divorce: Retaining a lawyer and starting divorce proceedings, only to lose your deposit when you reconcile.

Removing Names: Taking each other's names off joint accounts or assets, only to have to restore them later.

Changing Locks: Changing the locks on the house, only to give your spouse the new set later.

Staying Out All Night: Engaging in an affair, which leads to broken trust and a long road to repair if your spouse chooses to stay in the marriage.

Disrespectful Speech: Speaking disrespectfully about your spouse to family or friends, which can cause lasting damage to those relationships.

The Consequences of Angry Decisions

Decisions made in anger can cause more harm than the original argument. They can be costly, inconvenient, embarrassing, and deeply hurtful. It is far better to calm down before making any decisions. Often, once you have had a chance to cool off, you'll find that what you wanted to do in anger no longer seems like a good idea.

The Importance of Cooling Down

This principle is like the waiting period required in some states before purchasing a firearm. The cooling-off period gives you time to reconsider and calm down. Applying this rule to your relationship can prevent you from making rash decisions that could have lasting negative consequences.

Steps to Take

Pause and Reflect: When you are angry, take a moment to pause and think about your feelings.

Take Deep Breaths: Deep breathing can help calm your mind and body.

Seek Space: If necessary, take some time apart to cool down and gain perspective.

Reassess Your Feelings: After a few days, reassess your emotions. You may find that you feel differently once the anger has subsided.

Communicate: If the decision still feels right after you have cooled down, communicate it to your spouse calmly and respectfully.

Taking the time to cool down and think rationally before making decisions can help you avoid costly mistakes and work towards resolving conflicts in a healthier way. A calm mind leads to better decision-making and a stronger, more resilient relationship.

Physical and Verbal Abuse is Unacceptable

If you are in a physically abusive relationship, it is critical to seek help immediately. You do not need to protect your abuser—protect yourself and your children if you have them. There are several resources available in your local area to assist you.

Examples of Abuse:

- Pushing or shoving
- Slapping
- Spitting
- Choking
- Strong-arming (twisting body parts)
- Name-calling
- Tearing up belongings
- Destroying property
- Belittling
- Acts of intimidation
- Pinning down
- Use or brandishing of any weapon.

If you experience any of these forms of abuse, it is crucial to seek help immediately. Hotlines, shelters, and support groups are available to help you find safety and support. Remember, no one deserves abuse, and you have the right to live free from fear and harm.

Chapter 14

The Art of Effective Communication

Silence is Golden

Effective communication is not just about speaking; it often involves knowing when to be silent. Silence is a powerful tool in communication, conveying messages that words sometimes cannot. Whether it is expressing anger, a need for space, or simply showing respect by listening, silence plays a vital role in how we interact with our partners. This chapter will delve into the importance of respectful listening and how silence can be an essential part of effective communication.

The Power of Respectful Listening

There is an old saying: "Be quick to listen and slow to speak." This wisdom is especially crucial during disagreements. When you listen attentively, it shows a deep level of respect for your partner and their feelings. True listening often requires silence, allowing you to fully process what your partner is saying before responding. This approach not only prevents misunderstandings but also fosters a deeper connection and mutual respect in the relationship.

Benefits of Respectful Listening

Builds Respect: Listening attentively demonstrates respect for your partner's thoughts and opinions, even when you don't agree with them.

Enhances Understanding: By listening carefully, you gain a better understanding of your partner's perspective and emotions.

Reduces Conflict: Silence can help de-escalate intense arguments, reducing tension and stress in your relationship.

Improves Communication Skills: Practicing respectful listening helps both partners develop better communication skills, leading to more effective and meaningful conversations.

Practical Steps for Respectful Listening

- Be Present: When your partner is speaking, give them your full attention. Avoid distractions and focus entirely on their words and feelings.
- Maintain Eye Contact: Show that you are engaged and interested by maintaining eye contact. This non-verbal cue reinforces your attentiveness.
- Avoid Interrupting: Let your partner express themselves fully without interruption. Wait until they've finished before offering your thoughts.
- Acknowledge Their Words: Use small verbal cues or nods to

show that you are actively listening and processing what they
are saying.

- Process Before Responding: Take a moment to think about
  what your partner has said before you respond. This allows
  you to respond thoughtfully rather than react impulsively.

Handling Heated Arguments

During a heated argument, silence can be your ally. When your
partner is upset and shouting, it takes two people to escalate the conflict.
If you have the emotional strength to do so, remain silent while they
vent. This does not mean you are being passive; instead, it shows that
you are choosing to diffuse the situation rather than inflame it. When you
do speak, use a calm, low-pitched tone to help de-escalate the tension
and steer the conversation towards resolution.

The Role of Silence in Healing

On your journey to healing your marriage, managing how you
communicate is crucial. Silence can be a powerful tool for healing,
giving both partners the space to reflect and calm down before
addressing issues. By practicing respectful listening and strategically
using silence, you create a calmer, more supportive environment where
your relationship can rebuild and thrive.

Silence truly is golden when used effectively in communication. It
allows for respectful listening, reduces conflict, and enhances understanding between partners. By incorporating silence into your communication practices, you can develop stronger communication skills, build
respect, and foster a healthier, more peaceful relationship. Remember,
sometimes saying nothing at all can speak the loudest.

Manifestations of Frustration

Frustration in a relationship can manifest in many ways. The most common signs include separation, silence, withholding affection or communication, and frequent arguing. These behaviors often stem from deeper, unmet needs or unresolved issues. Anger and frustration are usually byproducts of something lacking or unfulfilled in a person's life. When these emotions are not addressed, they can lead to actions that create physical and emotional distance between partners.

The Importance of Addressing Issues

The best way to prevent frustration from escalating to physical separation is to talk through the issues before they reach a boiling point. Open, honest communication is essential to understanding each other's needs and resolving conflicts. Allowing conflicts to fester without addressing them is immature and unhealthy. It is crucial to understand the root cause of the frustration and work together to find a solution that brings you closer rather than pushing you apart.

A Cry for Help

When your partner retreats, it is often a cry for help—a sign that they need immediate attention to mend the relationship. Ignoring these signals can lead to further emotional and physical distance, making it even harder to repair the relationship later. This retreat isn't just about needing space; it is about feeling unheard and misunderstood. Addressing the issues head-on, with compassion and a genuine desire to improve the relationship, can make all the difference.

Strengthening the Bond

A healthy relationship requires effort, understanding, and a willingness to listen to each other's concerns. Don't let frustration drive a wedge between you and your partner. Instead, view these moments of tension as opportunities to grow closer and strengthen your bond. By addressing the underlying issues, fostering open communication, and being attentive to each other's needs, you can prevent the escalation that leads to physical separation and build a stronger, more resilient relationship.

Chapter 15

Watch Your Tone

Setting the Stage for Effective Communication

When you need to address a particular matter with your partner, it is essential to approach the conversation with the right mindset. The goal is not to argue but to communicate your concerns respectfully, without adding stress or tension to the situation. Many people avoid difficult conversations because they fear it may irritate or upset their partner. However, avoiding issues can lead to unresolved conflicts that fester and grow over time. A healthy relationship requires open dialogue, but how you approach that dialogue is key.

Timing and Tone Matter

Exercising wisdom in choosing the right words and the right time to talk is crucial. It is important to remember that your spouse is a person with emotions just like you. Speaking to them with the same level of respect you want to receive is fundamental to a productive conversation.

For example, if your partner has had a long, stressful day, it is not the best time to bring up a major issue. Instead, wait for a more appropriate moment—perhaps after they've had a chance to unwind, eat, take a shower, or relax with a glass of wine if that's their preference. Timing can significantly impact how your message is received. Both partners should feel comfortable enough to discuss concerns without feeling attacked or intimidated.

The Power of a Respectful Tone

Even if you are upset about the situation prompting the conversation, maintaining a respectful, low tone will help you communicate more effectively. When you approach your partner calmly, they're more likely to listen and respond positively. You might start the conversation by saying, "Honey, may I speak with you about something that's on my mind?" This softer approach can set a positive tone for the discussion, reducing any initial defensiveness or anxiety your partner might feel.

Avoiding Emotional Abuse

It is perfectly normal and healthy to address concerns in a relationship, but it is not okay to yell or scream at each other. Raising your voice and speaking harshly can quickly escalate into emotional abuse, which damages the relationship and creates a hostile environment. Instead, aim to keep your voice calm and your tone gentle. A soft tone can lead to a happier and more peaceful resolution, fostering understanding rather than conflict.

Why Your Tone Matters

How you say something is often more important than what you say. Your tone of voice can convey respect, love, and concern—or it can convey anger, frustration, and aggression. By watching your tone and speaking kindly, you make it easier for your partner to hear and understand your concerns. This approach does not just resolve the issue at hand; it strengthens overall communication and trust in your relationship.

So, next time you need to address an issue, remember to watch your tone. A respectful, gentle approach can make all the difference in how your conversation unfolds and in maintaining a healthy, loving relationship.

Chapter 16

Guarding Your Private Matters

The Importance of Privacy in Marriage

One of the biggest grievances in a marriage occurs when a spouse shares private matters with family and friends. This behavior is a form of betrayal, even if it does not involve cheating. Sharing intimate details of your relationship—especially those you know your spouse would not agree to share—constitutes a serious breach of trust. It is essential to recognize that some things are meant to remain between you and your partner, no matter how tempting it might be to seek outside support.

The Consequences of Sharing Private Matters

When you share sensitive information about your spouse, particularly with members of the opposite sex, it is not just a simple conversation—it is an act of disrespect, rudeness, and offensiveness. This behavior can create a greater wedge between you and your spouse, adding another layer of mistrust to an already volatile situation. Even if you feel justified in sharing because you are upset or hurt, it is crucial to consider the long-term impact on your relationship.

Respecting Your Partner's Privacy

It is perfectly normal to have friends you confide in, but it is important to choose wisely what you share. Ensure that what you discuss does not bring embarrassment or shame to your spouse. Some matters, especially those shared in confidence, should never be uttered to another person. When your spouse shares something with you in private, they trust you to keep it confidential. Violating that trust by sharing it with others can cause irreparable harm to your relationship.

The Dangers of a Smear Campaign

Sometimes, when partners are angry or believe the relationship is over, they may start a smear campaign against their spouse. This behavior is immature and disrespectful, and it is something I strongly advise against. Emotions can change, and many couples do work through their differences. However, if you have already spoken negatively about your spouse to others, reconciling becomes more complicated. Even if you and your spouse make amends, your family and friends may now view your partner with contempt based on the things you have said.

The Ripple Effect of Negative Talk

When you speak negatively about your spouse to others, you create a situation where not only do you both have to forgive each other, but your family members and friends must also find a way to forgive your spouse.

Unfortunately, while some may forgive, others may not. This is why it is so crucial to keep your family and friends out of your marital issues. Your lack of wisdom and maturity in this area can lead to divisions within families and cause unnecessary strain on in-law relationships.

Words Can't Be Taken Back

Once words are spoken, they can't be taken back. The seeds of contempt and mistrust you have planted in the hearts of your family and friends may take root and grow, making it difficult to restore peace even if your relationship heals. It is important to know what to share and what not to share to maintain the integrity of your marriage, whether you work things out or not. Keeping private matters private is a sign of maturity and respect for your partner.

Do It for Your Children

If you have children, maintaining a respectful and mature approach to your marital issues is even more critical. Children should not have a warped perception of their parents due to conflicts or negative talk. Even if you and your spouse aren't getting along, it is important to protect your children's view of their family. Never make decisions or speak out of anger because those actions are often the ones, you'll regret the most.

Protecting the Integrity of Your Marriage

Never bring your spouse to open shame or violate the integrity of your marriage, no matter the circumstances. Learning to deal with your marital issues maturely and respectfully is crucial for the health of your relationship and the well-being of your family. Guarding your private matters is not just about keeping secrets—it is about honoring the trust and bond you share with your partner.

Chapter 17

Conflict Resolution and Mediation

Unresolved Conflict

What is Conflict?

Conflict is a struggle or clash between opposing ideas, interests, or needs that are not easily reconciled. It is a natural part of any relationship, including marriage. Couples engage in conflicts every day —you are not alone. Conflicts can range from small, seemingly insignificant issues, like whose turn it is to pick up the kids or why the dry cleaning hasn't been collected, to more serious matters like questions of trust, financial responsibility, and lack of intimacy.

The Importance of Healthy Conflict Resolution

The key to maintaining a healthy relationship is learning how to navigate conflicts without damaging the person or the relationship. It is not about avoiding conflict altogether, but rather about addressing it in a way that is constructive rather than destructive. The mantra to live by is: talk it out, don't shout it out. While this may be difficult in the heat of the moment, it is achievable with practice and conscious effort.

Remember that the person you are in a relationship with has their own mind, thoughts, and feelings, which deserve respect, even if you don't agree with them. It is their right to have an opinion, and it is not your job to judge their thoughts as right or wrong. Mutual respect is crucial in any disagreement.

Addressing Conflict Immediately

When conflicts arise, they should be dealt with immediately—with sensitivity, compassion, and respect for your spouse's concerns, even if you feel that their argument is trivial. Respect their thoughts and opinions, because unresolved conflict can lead to more significant issues down the road. When conflicts are swept under the rug instead of being addressed, they can fester, leading to stress, anger, and aggravation in the future.

Unresolved conflict can prevent the healing and re-bonding process in a relationship. Problems that aren't dealt with will continue to resurface, sometimes in more intense forms. This is why it is important to handle conflicts promptly and effectively.

Effective Communication During Conflict

Listening is one of the most important aspects of conflict resolution. Allow your partner to speak without interruption. Over-talking or interrupting them shows a lack of respect for what they are trying to say and indicates that you are more concerned with making your own point than hearing theirs. This kind of behavior can escalate the conflict rather than resolve it.

It is helpful to establish communication rules early in your relationship. These rules might include allowing one person to speak without interruption and then yielding the floor to the other. You might also agree on a time limit for each person to speak, which can prevent the conversation from dragging on or becoming one-sided.

The Consequences of Unresolved Conflict

Unresolved conflict that lingers for days, weeks, or even months is like a decaying tooth—it only gets worse with time and can cause great pain later. When an issue arises, try to discuss it as soon as possible, ideally on the same day, and do so peacefully and respectfully. Try not to go to bed angry, if it can be avoided. Resolving conflicts promptly can prevent them from growing into bigger issues that are harder to resolve.

For conflicts that are more serious or deeply rooted, it may be necessary to seek help from a professional therapist or marriage counselor. While conflict resolution can be challenging, it is entirely possible when both partners are committed to the process and willing to practice good communication habits.

The Path to Resolution

Conflicts can be resolved effectively when both partners are mature and willing to understand each other's concerns. It takes effort, patience, and commitment to the relationship to navigate conflicts in a healthy way. By addressing issues as they arise, listening with respect, and working together to find solutions, you can prevent unresolved conflicts from damaging your relationship and build a stronger, more resilient bond with your partner.

Chapter 18

We Need a Mediator

When Couples Can't Find Common Ground

When a couple struggles to find common ground, see eye to eye, or resolve their issues independently, it does not necessarily mean the relationship is doomed. Many couples, unfortunately, are quick to conclude that their relationship is heading toward dissolution, rather than seeking the right kind of help that could steer them back on track. In these situations, it is all too easy to blame your partner for the failures in the marriage without acknowledging your own role in the problems. It is not uncommon for one partner to believe they've done nothing wrong, contributing to the impasse. This is often a clear sign that it is time to seek help from a qualified marital coach or mediator.

The Importance of an Outside Perspective

Have you ever noticed that during a debate with your partner, you almost always believe you are right? This is a natural inclination, but it can be a significant barrier to resolving conflicts. Sometimes, getting an outside perspective on the issue can help you see things more clearly and recognize where you might be contributing to the problem. A mediator can provide that neutral, third-party viewpoint, offering insights that neither of you may have considered.

However, it is crucial to seek this outside perspective from the right person. A professional relationship coach or counselor is often the best option because they are trained to handle these situations impartially and with the expertise needed to guide you through your challenges.

Caution Against Sharing with the Wrong People

While it is beneficial to get another person's point of view, you must be very selective about whom you choose to confide in. Sharing intimate details of your marriage with gossiping family members or friends can do more harm than good. Not everyone has the wisdom or the best intentions when offering advice, and some may inadvertently (or intentionally) cause further strain on your relationship.

Involving family and friends can also lead to long-term issues, especially if they develop negative opinions about your spouse based on what you have shared. It is important to protect the integrity of your marriage by being cautious about what you disclose and to whom.

Trusted Support When a Mediator Isn't Available

If a professional marriage coach isn't available, having a trusted friend or close family member to talk to can be helpful. However, it is essential to exercise extreme wisdom in these situations. Share your concerns in a way that does not bring shame or humiliation to your spouse or your marriage. Avoid spreading contempt or planting seeds of negativity in the hearts of those you confide in. Remember, your goal is to find resolution and healing, not to create more division.

The Role of a Mediator

A mediator's role is to help you, and your partner communicate more effectively, find common ground, and work through your issues with respect and understanding. They can help you see each other's perspectives more clearly and guide you toward solutions that you might not have discovered on your own. Seeking mediation is not a sign of failure; rather, it is a proactive step towards saving and strengthening your marriage.

By involving a mediator or trusted advisor, you are taking an important step towards resolution. This approach can help you and your partner move past your differences and build a stronger, more resilient relationship.

Chapter 19

Moving Past Mistakes and Betrayal

Understanding Betrayal

Betrayal is a profound violation of trust or confidence. It is not just about infidelity; betrayal can take many forms, each of which can deeply wound a relationship. Understanding the various ways betrayal can manifest is the first step in addressing it within your marriage.

Common Forms of Betrayal

1. **Cheating:**Engaging in a physical or emotional affair outside the marriage.
2. **Revealing Secrets:**Sharing private matters of your relationship with others.
3. **Emotional Affair:**Forming a deep emotional connection with someone outside the marriage.
4. **Lying:**Being dishonest about important matters.
5. **Disrespect:**Treating your spouse with a lack of respect and consideration.

6. **Neglect:**Ignoring your spouse's needs and the needs of the relationship.
7. **Keeping Secrets:**Hiding significant information from your spouse.
8. **Double-Crossing:**Betraying your spouse's trust in significant ways.
9. **Harmful Disclosure:**Disclosing confidential information that harms your spouse.
10. **Dishonesty:**Not being truthful in various aspects of the relationship.
11. **Gaslighting:**Manipulating your spouse into doubting their own perceptions and sanity.

The Impact of Betrayal

Infidelity and other forms of betrayal are agonizing experiences that can bring intense feelings of embarrassment, shame, guilt, grief, depression, and anxiety. Couples who survive betrayal do so through hard work, dedication, and often, faith. The offending partner must commit to showing extreme transparency, free from pride or arrogance, and be willing to do whatever it takes to regain their partner's trust.

Tips for Surviving Betrayal

1. **Attend Couples Therapy/Coaching:**Seek professional help to navigate the healing process together.
2. **Talk About the Affair:**Openly discuss the betrayal to understand what went wrong and address underlying issues.
3. **Figure Out What Went Wrong:**Identify the root causes of the betrayal and work on resolving them.

4. **Build Trust:**Methodically plan out steps to rebuild trust, such as being transparent and consistent.
5. **Practice Self-Care:**Both partners should take care of their emotional and physical well-being.
6. **Forgiveness:**Work towards forgiving each other to move past the betrayal.
7. **Don't Do It Again:**The offending partner must commit to never repeating the betrayal.

Moving Past Betrayal

Moving past betrayal is one of the most challenging things a couple can face, but it is attainable depending on your capacity to forgive, let go, and the strength of your love and commitment to your partner. Healing is possible if the betrayal was not a habitual behavior and if your partner is genuinely remorseful, with actions to validate that their betrayal was a mistake.

Making a Choice

If you find that you cannot forgive or move past your partner's betrayal, it may be best to end the relationship. Holding onto a relationship where forgiveness isn't possible will keep you both trapped in a cycle of hurt and bitterness, turning your relationship toxic. Before making any decisions, consider counseling to explore all options and strive for a positive outcome.

The Power of Forgiveness

Forgiveness is a powerful choice that can shape the future of your relationship. No one is perfect, and we all make mistakes. If you decide to forgive, it is important to remember that forgiveness can lead to healing and growth. However, holding onto grudges can perpetuate pain and resentment. Give your spouse the grace and mercy you would want to receive if the roles were reversed.

If your relationship is worth saving, then do what it takes to help both of you heal and strengthen your bond. But if the betrayal continues and you see no chance of recovery, seek counsel and make the decision that best serves your well-being and happiness.

Chapter 20

Don't Keep Repeating the Same Mistakes

Understanding the Need for Change

We are all imperfect human beings who make mistakes and missteps. At times, we all need forgiveness for something we've said or done that hurt someone else. However, when it comes to marriage, building trust and confidence in each other means that certain mistakes should not be repeated. A mistake that is constantly repeated isn't just a mistake anymore—it becomes a choice or a decision you are making.

The Importance of Avoiding Repeated Mistakes

As you embark on your marriage rewind journey, it is crucial to avoid the mistakes and offenses you have been guilty of in the past. True repentance and genuine sorrow for your actions are shown through real, changed behavior. You can't keep apologizing for the same offense and then continue to repeat it. When you repeatedly violate your spouse's trust with intolerable actions, it causes them to lose confidence in you as a person, and your words will lose their value.

The Value of Your Words

A person's word holds value only when they honor it by standing by what they say, even when it is uncomfortable. If you consistently repeat the same offense, your spouse will find it difficult, if not impossible, to trust anything you say. This leads to frustration, irritation, and anger, compounding the issues in an already strained relationship.

The Consequences of Repeated Mistakes

There's nothing more frustrating than desperately wanting your marriage to get back on track, believing it is heading in the right direction, only to be let down by a spouse who can't seem to control themselves or the behavior causing harm in the marriage. This continued pattern can cause further damage and devastation, leading to the gradual deterioration of the relationship if left unchecked.

Strategies to Avoid Repeating Mistakes

1. **Self-Reflection:** Take time to reflect on your actions and understand the root cause of your mistakes. Awareness is the first step toward change.
2. **Seek Help:** If you find it difficult to change certain behaviors on your own, seek help through counseling or talk to a trusted advisor, such as a pastor, if your area person of faith.

3. **Be Intentional:**Approach your marriage rewind journey with a focused and intentional mindset. Be prepared to do whatever it takes to help heal and mend your relationship.
4. **Change Behavior:**True repentance is shown through changed behavior. Demonstrate to your spouse that you are serious about making positive changes by consistently acting differently.
5. **Accountability:**Hold yourself accountable and ask your spouse to help keep you accountable. This mutual support can be crucial in preventing repeated mistakes.
6. **Consistent Effort:**Understand that rebuilding trust takes time and dedication. Make a consistent effort to avoid repeating past mistakes and to show your spouse that you are committed to change.

The Road to Healing

While your marriage is in rewind mode, it is essential to avoid falling back into old patterns of behavior. If you struggle to get a handle on your issues, don't hesitate to seek professional help or guidance. The goal is to rebuild trust and create a strong, healthy relationship that can withstand future challenges.

Remember, a successful marriage rewind journey requires intentional actions and a genuine commitment to change. Avoiding repeated mistakes is crucial for rebuilding trust and laying the foundation for a lasting, loving relationship. The effort you put in will be worth it!

Chapter 21

Forgiveness and Apology

When You Realize You Should Apologize

In the landscape of a marriage, some conflicts can be resolved with something as simple and powerful as an apology. A heartfelt "I am sorry" can work wonders, sometimes diffusing a situation before it spirals into an unnecessary argument. I've learned in my own marriage that not every issue needs to be debated or turned into a drawn-out discussion. Often, it is not what you said that causes a problem, but how you said it. The tone and delivery of your words can either calm the waters or stir up a storm.

Apologizing is an act of humility. It sends a clear message to your partner: "I love you and value our relationship more than my need to be right." There was a time in my marriage when we were learning to navigate our conflicts with more maturity and respect. I was incredibly upset over something my husband had done, and in my frustration, I reacted in a way that was less than respectful. Instead of escalating the situation, my husband approached me calmly, wrapped his arms around me, kissed me on the forehead, and asked me to take a breath and calm down. His response completely disarmed me. I immediately felt the tension leave the room, and we were able to talk things through peacefully. It was a moment of learning for both of us—a real-life example of how powerful a calm, loving response can be when emotions are running high.

The Power of a Simple Apology

Saying to your partner, "I am sorry, please forgive me. I didn't mean to upset you," can be incredibly effective in fostering a healthy, long-lasting relationship. Sometimes, letting go of the need to argue your point in favor of preserving peace can be the best choice. It is not about conceding defeat but about prioritizing harmony and love in your relationship over the need to be right.

In a marriage, it is important to remember that your spouse is not your enemy. They are the person you chose to spend your life with, the person you vowed to love and cherish through all the ups and downs. Keeping this perspective can help you both overcome challenges that might otherwise threaten to erode your relationship. Don't lose sight of the love and commitment that brought you together in the first place.

When you recognize that you have hurt your partner, whether intentionally or not, a sincere apology can mend the rift before it widens. It shows that you are willing to take responsibility for your actions and that you care about your partner's feelings. Apologizing does not make you weak—it makes you strong enough to put your relationship first.

Building a Culture of Apology and Forgiveness

A healthy relationship thrives on a foundation of mutual respect, love, and the willingness to apologize when necessary. Saying "I am sorry" and asking for forgiveness should be a regular practice in any marriage. It is a sign that you value your partner and the life you are building together. This simple act can prevent small issues from becoming major problems and help you both move on quickly from conflicts.

Moreover, an apology opens the door to forgiveness. When one partner apologizes sincerely, it encourages the other to respond with grace and understanding. This back-and-forth of apology and forgiveness creates a safe space in the relationship where both partners feel valued and respected, even when mistakes are made.

Remember, you both are worth the effort it takes to maintain and nurture a healthy, loving relationship. Apologizing and forgiving are essential tools in this journey. The next time you find yourself at odds with your spouse, try setting aside your pride and simply say, "I am sorry." You might be surprised at how quickly the tension dissolves and how much stronger your relationship becomes as a result.

Chapter 22

Be Prepared to Forgive Often

The Necessity of Forgiveness in Marriage

Marriage is a journey shared between two imperfect people, and along the way, mistakes will inevitably happen. If you are married to another human being, it is essential to maintain a posture of forgiveness throughout your relationship. Offenses will come, but what truly matters is how you handle those offenses—maturely, respectfully, and with a heart ready to forgive.

Imagine you and your partner each wearing a backpack filled with little white notecards that read in bold print: "Forgive me" or "I forgive you." Every time your partner offends you, you reach into your backpack and hand them one of these cards. This simple, symbolic act highlights the crucial role forgiveness plays in keeping a marriage healthy and enduring.

The Importance of Forgiveness

Forgiving your partner frequently is one of the keys to a long-lasting and fulfilling relationship. Holding onto grudges or past offenses only serves to breed resentment and creates barriers between you and your spouse. In contrast, practicing forgiveness allows you to extend the same mercy and grace that you would want to receive. It might not be easy at first, but like any skill, forgiveness becomes easier with practice.

Steps to Practicing Forgiveness

1. **Acknowledge the Hurt:**Recognize and accept that you have been hurt by your partner's actions or words. Acknowledgment is the first step toward healing.
2. **Communicate Your Feelings:**Share your feelings with your spouse calmly and respectfully. Use "I" statements to express how their actions affected you, avoiding blame or accusations. This approach opens a pathway for understanding rather than defense.
3. **Choose to Forgive:**Forgiveness is a conscious choice. Decide to let go of the hurt and resentment and commit to moving forward together.
4. **Give a Forgiveness Card:**Whether symbolically or literally, offer your partner a "Forgive me" or "I forgive you" card. This gesture reinforces your decision to forgive and sets a positive tone for reconciliation.
5. **Let Go of the Past:**Once you have forgiven, truly let go of past offenses. Don't bring them up in future disagreements or use them as a weapon against your spouse. Holding onto past grievances only keeps you both stuck in a cycle of hurt.
6. **Focus on the Positive:**Shift your focus to the positive aspects

of your relationship and your partner's good qualities. This helps rebuild trust and strengthens your bond.

7. **Practice Empathy:**Try to put yourself in your partner's shoes and understand their perspective. Empathy fosters compassion and helps you see the situation from their point of view, making forgiveness easier.

8. **Reiterate Your Commitment:**After forgiving, reaffirm your commitment to your spouse and your relationship. Let them know that you are dedicated to working through challenges together, reinforcing the foundation of your marriage.

The Benefits of Forgiveness

Practicing forgiveness brings numerous benefits to your marriage:

- **Emotional Healing:**Forgiveness allows you to heal emotionally, reducing feelings of anger and bitterness. It is a way to cleanse the emotional wounds that would otherwise fester and grow.
- **Strengthened Relationship:**A forgiving attitude strengthens the bond between you and your spouse, creating a deeper sense of trust and intimacy. This bond makes it easier to weather future storms together.
- **Reduced Stress:**Carrying grudges is emotionally and physically taxing. Forgiveness promotes a sense of peace and reduces stress, allowing you to focus on the positives in your relationship.
- **Improved Communication:**Forgiveness opens the door for honest and open communication. When both partners know they're operating in a space of forgiveness, they feel safer expressing themselves without fear of retribution.

Forgiveness in Action

Forgiveness may not come easily at first, but it becomes more natural with practice. Just as you would practice any skill to improve, practicing forgiveness can make it a more effortless and integral part of your relationship. It is important to remember that forgiveness is a gift you give to yourself as much as to your spouse. It frees you from the heavy burden of anger and allows you to focus on building a loving and harmonious relationship.

By maintaining a posture of forgiveness, you create an environment where love and understanding can flourish. Be prepared to forgive often, and you'll find that your relationship grows stronger and more resilient over time. Through forgiveness, you cultivate a marriage that can withstand the inevitable challenges that life will throw your way, allowing your love to deepen and endure.

Chapter 23

Don't Be Dismissive in Conversations

The Importance of Listening

In any marriage, communication is key, and a significant part of effective communication is attentive listening. Often, we underestimate how much a conflict can be diffused simply by listening to our partner—even when we don't agree with what they're saying. It is perfectly okay not to agree with your spouse's perspective. The saying, "We can agree to disagree," is important to keep in mind. What matters most is allowing your partner the space to voice their thoughts, opinions, and concerns without being dismissive or invalidating their feelings.

Respectful Communication

Being dismissive is a clear sign of disrespect. It sends a strong message that you don't value your partner's opinion on a certain topic or situation. This can deeply wound your spouse and create barriers in your relationship. It is essential to let your partner express what they're feeling without interrupting or dismissing their thoughts. Show patience and understanding, just as you would want them to do for you. Couples should practice yielding to each other in conversations, allowing room for both voices to be heard. While this can be challenging at first, consistent effort will lead to better communication and a more respectful dynamic between you both.

Managing Heated Arguments

During heated arguments, it is common to want to talk over the person you are speaking with, which can be incredibly frustrating and unproductive. When you find yourself in this situation, take a moment to calm down. Let your partner speak, and then interject when it is your turn. If your partner isn't allowing you to get a word in, calmly ask, "Can I speak now?" Using a soft-spoken tone can help manage the situation positively and defuse the tension in the room. This approach requires maturity and growth—someone needs to be the bigger person, and it might as well be you.

Making Your Partner Feel Heard

Making your partner feel heard is crucial for healthy communication. After they've finished speaking, calmly acknowledge their perspective by saying something like, "I hear what you are saying, and I respect your point of view, but I must respectfully add..." This approach shows that you value their opinion, even if you disagree. It also builds your partner's confidence to speak openly with you, knowing they won't be met with dismissiveness or anger. Creating a safe space for communication is essential, especially as you work through your marriage rewind journey. Remember to be kind, respectful, patient, understanding, and calm in your conversations.

Examples of Dismissive Behavior

- **Showing no interest** in what your partner is saying
- **Pretending** their concerns aren't valid
- **Giving short answers** or refusing to engage in the conversation
- **Interrupting** them while they're speaking
- **Ignoring** their input or brushing it off as unimportant

Dismissive Phrases to Avoid

- "Never mind."
- "You just can't leave it alone."
- "That's just the way it is."
- "Get over it."
- "Why does it even matter?"
- "What difference does it make?"
- "Whatever."
- "That's just silly."
- "I don't have time for this."
- "You are overreacting."
- "That's not important."
- "Can we talk about something else?"
- "I've heard that before."

Actions of a Dismissive Person

- **Walking away** while your partner is talking
- **Not making eye contact**

- **Displaying body language** that suggests they're being bothered
- **Smirking** or showing disrespect through facial expressions
- **Engaging in other activities** while your partner is trying to talk
- **Ignoring** your partner entirely
- **Speaking negatively** about everything they say
- **Trying to intimidate** your partner into silence

Characteristics of a Dismissive Person

- They **never apologize**.
- They **belittle** or mock your opinions.
- They **don't take you seriously**.
- They **discount your feelings**.
- They are **judgmental**.
- They always think they're **right**.
- They become **defensive** when confronted.
- They **never take accountability** for their actions.

Addressing Dismissive Behavior

If you notice these behaviors in yourself or your partner, it is important to address them respectfully. Being dismissive can harm your relationship, so bring it to your partner's attention if they exhibit these behaviors. Express how you feel and assert your needs or opinions clearly, firmly, but with respect. Sometimes, people aren't even aware that they're being dismissive because they've grown up in environments where this behavior was the norm. By addressing it, you are not only helping them grow as a person but also fostering better communication between you both, which in turn will help build a healthier, stronger relationship.

Being dismissive may seem like a small issue, but it can have a significant impact on the health of your relationship. Learning to listen attentively, respond thoughtfully, and communicate with respect is crucial to keeping your marriage strong and resilient. By avoiding dismissiveness and making your partner feel heard, you create a foundation of trust and mutual respect that will help your relationship thrive.

Praise in Public, Rebuke in Private

One of the most important principles in a marriage is to never correct or criticize your spouse in front of others, regardless of what they have done or said in public. Honor and respect are paramount, both in private and public settings. If your spouse offends you or does something inappropriate in public, the best approach is to quietly and discreetly pull them aside. Address the issue respectfully and privately, without drawing unnecessary attention or causing shame and embarrassment.

Praising your spouse in public, on the other hand, is a powerful way to build them up and reinforce your commitment to each other. Public praise demonstrates that you value and appreciate your spouse, which strengthens your bond and boosts their confidence. It can be as simple as complimenting their appearance, expressing gratitude for something they've done, or acknowledging their achievements. These small acts of public recognition not only uplift your spouse but also set a positive example for others.

Criticizing your spouse in public, however, can have serious negative consequences. It can lead to feelings of humiliation, resentment, and a breakdown of trust. Public criticism often creates a hostile environment and may cause your spouse to become defensive or withdraw emotionally. By addressing any issues privately, you show your spouse that you respect their dignity and that you value your relationship enough to handle conflicts in a way that preserves their self-esteem.

Tips for Practicing This Principle

1. **Praise Often:** Make it a regular habit to speak highly of your spouse in front of others. Share your appreciation for their qualities and actions, which reinforces positive behavior and creates a supportive environment.
2. **Choose the Right Time:** If you need to address an issue, select a time when both of you are calm and away from public view. This ensures the conversation remains productive and not influenced by the presence of others.
3. **Use Positive Language:** When discussing sensitive topics, focus on the behavior rather than the person. For example, instead of saying, "You always embarrass me," you could say, "I felt embarrassed when this happened." This approach helps maintain the conversation's focus on resolving the issue rather than assigning blame.
4. **Stay Calm:** Approach conversations with a calm and composed demeanor. Staying calm helps prevent the situation from escalating and shows your spouse that you are genuinely concerned about resolving the issue, not just venting your frustrations.
5. **Express Understanding:** Show empathy by acknowledging your spouse's feelings and perspective. Work together to find a solution that respects both of your viewpoints.
6. **Follow Up:** After addressing an issue, follow up with positive reinforcement. Let your spouse know you appreciate their efforts to improve and that you are committed to supporting them in the future.

Practicing the principle of praising in public and rebuking in private helps build a foundation of mutual respect and trust in your marriage. This approach allows both partners to feel valued and understood, fostering a healthy and loving relationship that can withstand the challenges of life.

Chapter 24

Nurturing Your Relationship is Vital

What Does It Mean to Nurture?

To nurture means to care for and encourage the growth of something or someone. In the context of marriage, nurturing your relationship involves consistently investing time, energy, and love into each other to ensure that your bond remains strong and healthy. Are you both nurturing your relationship? This is a question every couple should ask themselves regularly.

Essential Practices for Nurturing Your Relationship

1. **Communicate a Lot:** Regular, open communication is the lifeblood of any strong relationship. It helps you stay connected and understand each other's needs, desires, and concerns.
2. **Be Honest and Faithful:** Trust is the foundation of a strong marriage. Build and maintain trust through honesty and faithfulness.

3. **Be There for One Another:** Whether in times of joy or sorrow, being a source of support for each other strengthens your bond.
4. **Leave the Past in the Past:** Holding onto past mistakes only hinders growth. Focus on the present and future, allowing past grievances to remain where they belong—in the past.
5. **Don't Fear Conflict:** Conflict is inevitable, but it does not have to be destructive. Address conflicts head-on and use them as opportunities for growth.
6. **Touch:** Physical affection, such as holding hands, hugging, and kissing, strengthens your emotional connection.
7. **Appreciate One Another:** Regularly express gratitude and appreciation for each other. Acknowledging the small things can make a big difference.
8. **Be Best Friends:** Cultivate a deep friendship within your marriage. Being each other's confidant and companion creates a solid foundation.
9. **Unconditional Love:** Love your spouse without conditions or expectations. This kind of love fosters security and stability.
10. **Stay Connected:** Make efforts to stay emotionally and physically connected. Prioritize spending quality time together.
11. **Affirm Each Other Often:** Regularly affirm and complement each other. Positive reinforcement strengthens the relationship.
12. **Encourage Individuality:** Support each other's personal growth and interests. A healthy marriage allows both partners to flourish as individuals.
13. **Trust Each Other:** Trust is crucial. Build it, maintain it, and don't let it be eroded by doubts or insecurities.
14. **Create Time for Romance:** Romance shouldn't fade over time. Be intentional about creating time for romance, separate from work and family obligations.
15. **Grow Together:** Don't stop growing together as a couple.

Embrace changes and challenges as opportunities to deepen your connection.

16. **Avoid Bad Habits:**Don't let bad habits sneak into your relationship, especially during tough times. Fight to stay connected, even when you are tempted to pull away.

17. **Renew Excitement:**Regularly find ways to bring excitement into your relationship. New experiences can rekindle the spark.

18. **Time Management:**Learn to manage time effectively between your relationship, work, and family. Creating balance is essential to avoid neglect.

19. **Check In:**Don't assume your spouse is okay. Regularly check in with each other about how you are feeling and what you need.

20. **Remove Negative Influences:**Identify and eliminate any negative influences in your marriage, whether they're people, habits, or external pressures.

Dealing with Unwanted Influences

What if your spouse is friends or in business with someone you don't like? This situation can be tricky, but it is essential to approach it with care and consideration.

Questions to Ask:

1. **Infidelity:**Has there been evidence of infidelity, inappropriate conversations, or actions?

2. **Disrespect:**Has the friend been disrespectful to you in any way?

3. **Past Relationships:**Was your spouse in a previous relationship with this friend or co-worker?
4. **Sabotage:**Is this friend or co-worker trying to sabotage your marriage?
5. **Contempt:**Does this person openly show dislike or contempt towards your spouse?

If any of these issues are present, your spouse likely has valid reasons for disliking this person. In such cases, if you value your marriage over the friendship, it may be in your best interest to distance yourself from this friend. However, if your spouse's feelings stem from jealousy, insecurity, or trust issues without any concrete evidence of wrongdoing, it is important to approach the situation differently.

Steps to Resolve Conflicts About Friendships

1. **Respectful Discussions:**Instead of fighting over the issue, discuss it maturely and respectfully. Understanding each other's perspectives is key.
2. **Loyalty to Spouse:**Your loyalty to your spouse should come first. Their feelings and concerns should be taken seriously and worked out properly.
3. **Affirm Your Spouse:**Make sure your spouse feels valued and important above all else. Reassure them that they are the most important person in your life.
4. **Compromise:**If cutting off a friendship brings your spouse peace, consider doing it without argument. If the friendship is important to you, consider reducing the time spent with that friend until your spouse feels more secure.
5. **Counseling:**If trust issues are the root cause, and there have been no prior offenses, consider counseling to help your

spouse work through their insecurities. Addressing the underlying causes is crucial for healing.

Maintaining Long-Lasting Friendships

While your spouse is on their journey to healing, communicate with your friends (with your spouse's permission) about the situation to avoid hurt feelings. If your spouse is uncomfortable with sharing their issues, be creative in maintaining the integrity of long-lasting friendships without causing friction in your marriage.

Nurturing your relationship requires effort, understanding, and prioritizing each other above all else. By practicing these principles, you can create a healthy and thriving marriage that withstands the test of time and external pressures.

Hug Therapy

Can you imagine the power of a simple hug? A hug can disarm even the toughest person and melt away tension in moments of conflict. Many disputes or misunderstandings with your partner can be resolved with just a hug. A hug is a language all its own, speaking volumes without uttering a single word. When you approach your partner with a hug during an argument, it sends a signal to their brain to pause and reassess. A hug can change the trajectory of a situation, diffusing tension and confusion about what to do next.

A hug says, "I know you are angry, but I love you, and I don't want to fight." It brings peace and solace, serving as a gentle reminder that the relationship is more important than the conflict. A hug can seize the moment, take charge of the atmosphere in your home, and bring it back to a state of peace before things get out of hand. This isn't about dismissing your partner's concerns; rather, it is about creating a safe space to address those concerns calmly and respectfully. Once you have used a hug to set a peaceful tone, you can move forward with the conversation in a more constructive way.

Recognizing Warning Signs

Understanding the warning signs of an impending argument with your partner can help you take preemptive action. When you recognize these signs, you have a choice: you can either escalate the situation by responding in anger, or you can choose to diffuse it with a well-timed hug.

Warning Signs Include

- Getting unusually quiet
- Displaying an attitude
- Experiencing sudden mood changes
- Withdrawing from usual activities
- Giving off a negative vibe
- Ignoring or avoiding interaction
- Eye rolling or other dismissive gestures
- Pretending everything is fine when it clearly isn't
- Trouble sleeping or signs of depression

Medical Benefits of Hugging

Hugging is not just emotionally beneficial; it also has numerous proven medical benefits:

- **Stress Reduction:**Hugs release oxytocin, the "love" hormone, which helps people feel bonded and connected. This hormone can also activate relaxation responses, reducing stress levels by lowering cortisol and norepinephrine, other stress hormones.
- **Improving Heart Health:**Hugs can lower blood pressure and heart rate, improving cardiovascular function and reducing the risk of heart-related issues.
- **Reducing Inflammation:**Hugging can help reduce inflammation, which is the body's response to stress and illness. It can even help fight infections and reduce the severity of the common cold.
- **Increasing Feelings of Safety and Belonging:**Hugs make people feel more connected, which fosters communication and emotional security.
- **Improving Sleep:**The chemicals released during a hug, such as oxytocin, serotonin, and dopamine, can improve sleep quality, which is vital for overall health.
- **Providing Pain Relief:**Hugs can temporarily reduce chronic pain, offering comfort and relief.
- **Supporting Muscle Regeneration:**Hugs can contribute to muscle regeneration and recovery, adding to their overall health benefits.

Hugging for a Healthy Marriage

While I'm not a medical doctor, I highly recommend a daily dose of hugs to help reduce the stress and anxiety in your relationship, bringing you and your partner closer to a healthy marriage. Hugging can also improve your overall health—physically, mentally, emotionally, and spiritually. It is important to find balance in your life—mind, body, soul, and spirit. When all these elements align within both of you, there's nothing you can't accomplish together as a united force!

A hug might seem simple, but its impact can be profound. It is a tool for healing, for connection, and for showing love in a way that words sometimes can't. Incorporating hug therapy into your daily routine can help ensure that your marriage thrives, offering a comforting reminder of your love and commitment to one another.

Laughter Works Like Medicine - A Couple That Laughs Together Stays Together

Laughter is often described as the best medicine, and there's a good reason for that. Not only does it bring joy and lightness to our lives, but science also suggests that laughter has a multitude of benefits that can improve our mental, physical, cognitive, and social health. When it comes to marriage, laughter can be a powerful tool to strengthen your bond, defuse conflicts, and enhance the overall quality of your relationship.

Chapter 25

What Science Says About Laughter

Mental Health: Laughter is a natural mood booster. It can help reduce stress, depression, and anxiety by increasing levels of dopamine and serotonin, which are neurotransmitters that contribute to emotional well-being. When you laugh, your brain releases endorphins, the body's natural feel-good chemicals, which create a sense of happiness and relaxation.

Physical Health: Laughter has been shown to reduce pain by raising pain thresholds, acting as a natural analgesic. It also improves blood flow and oxygen intake, which can lower cortisol levels, the hormone associated with stress. This helps the body relax, reducing physical tension and boosting the immune system.

Cognitive Function: Laughter can enhance cognitive functions such as problem-solving, creativity, and mental clarity. When you laugh, your brain receives a burst of activity that sharpens your ability to think clearly and approach problems from different angles.

Social Health: Laughter is a powerful social tool that strengthens relationships, promotes teamwork, and helps to defuse conflicts. It is also contagious—when one person starts laughing, it often spreads through a group, creating a sense of togetherness and safety. Laughter fosters an environment of openness and connection, making it easier to bond with others.

Laughter and Social Health in Your Marriage

Let's dive deeper into how laughter specifically enhances the social health of your marriage. In the social context of a relationship, laughter serves as a bridge between partners, helping to break down walls and create a space where both can feel safe and accepted.

Laughing With, Not At: Socially speaking, it is not just about laughing at each other's quirks or mistakes, but rather laughing together. When couples laugh together, it builds a stronger bond of friendship and partnership. Unfortunately, many couples take themselves and each other too seriously, forgetting the simple joy of shared laughter. It is particularly hard to laugh when you are constantly at odds but breaking that cycle of over-seriousness can transform your relationship.

How Laughter Strengthens Bonds: Couples who laugh together tend to have stronger, more resilient relationships. Laughter helps to soften the edges of conflict, making it easier to address issues without escalating them. It is a reminder that, at the end of the day, your relationship is built on love, friendship, and shared experiences. Laughter creates a positive feedback loop—when you laugh together, you feel closer, and when you feel closer, you laugh more easily.

Practical Ways to Bring Laughter into Your Marriage
Incorporating laughter into your marriage does not have to be complicated. Here are some simple and fun ways to start:

- **Watch Comedy Together:**Whether it is a comedy movie, a stand-up special, or a funny TV show, find something that makes you both laugh and enjoy it together.

- **Attend Comedy Events:**Look for local comedy shows or events where you can laugh together in a social setting. The shared experience of live laughter can be incredibly bonding.
- **Play Silly Games:**Engage in playful activities like paintball, visiting amusement parks, or even having a pillow fight. The goal is to be silly together and create memories that you'll laugh about for years to come.
- **Create Your Own Fun:**You don't need to rely on external activities to bring laughter into your relationship. My husband and I have a quirky game we play after watching movies. As the movie nears its end, whoever thinks of it first tries to beat the other to the bedroom. It is a race to grab our belongings, shout something silly, and dash to the bed. The winner gets to relax while the loser must shut everything off and lock the doors. This spontaneous game always has us laughing hysterically, and it is just one of many ways we keep the fun alive in our marriage.

The Importance of Shared Laughter

The story I shared illustrates how couples can create their own moments of laughter. It does not have to make sense to anyone else; it just must make you both happy. Laughter is an expression of love and joy that does not need to be complicated or planned. It is about being authentic, enjoying each other's company, and finding humor in the little things.

Life is too short to be serious all the time. Imagine how deeply you would feel the loss if something were to happen to your spouse. The memories of shared laughter and joy will be what sustains you through difficult times. Laughter helps to strengthen your union and friendship, making your marriage more resilient and fulfilling.

So, make it a point to laugh, laugh, and laugh some more. Seek out opportunities to bring joy into your relationship, and don't be afraid to be a little silly together. After all, a couple that laughs together truly does stay together.

I Should Feel Safe with You

The greatest feeling in the world is being in a relationship with someone you can truly trust—someone whose life is an open book, free from secrets, betrayal, and dishonesty. When you are with a partner who makes you feel emotionally safe, you can let your guard down and feel secure in the relationship. However, if your spouse is constantly suspicious of you because of a history of inappropriate behaviors that haven't changed, it can lead to a sense of emotional insecurity. Even if you have sworn to change, your partner might still have that nagging voice in their head, wondering what you might be doing behind closed doors.

No one wants to be in a relationship with someone they can't trust or feel unsafe with. It is even more troubling if a spouse wants to leave but feels trapped due to financial insecurities or other constraints. There are countless things that can make a partner feel unsafe in a relationship, and these concerns should be taken seriously for the health of your marriage.

Understanding the Signs

One clear sign that your spouse feels unsafe is when they experience anxiety every time your phone rings or a text message notification goes off. This reaction often stems from something that's been discovered before—something that triggered a sense of unease and distrust. If your spouse feels this way, it is a clue that something in the relationship needs to be fixed.

For example, you could grant your spouse access to your phone or allow them to answer calls for you. This simple act can alleviate their anxiety and demonstrate that you have nothing to hide. However, if your spouse is uncomfortable with the idea of you having access to their phone, it might indicate that something suspicious is going on. Often, a spouse who refuses to be transparent might be hiding something— whether it is inappropriate behavior on social media, secret bank accounts, or other secrets that could damage the relationship.

In a healthy, transparent relationship, there should be no need to hide anything. Remember when landline phones were the norm, and anyone nearby could answer a ringing phone? What's the problem with your spouse answering your phone now? It is something worth thinking about.

Behaviors That Promote Safety and Trust

If you want your spouse to feel safe and secure with you, here are some behaviors that can help:

- **Allow Phone Access:**Being open with your phone shows transparency and builds trust.
- **Be Open and Transparent:**Share your thoughts, feelings, and actions openly.
- **Hold No Secrets:**Keeping secrets only breeds distrust and insecurity.
- **Be Honest:**Always tell the truth, even when it is difficult.
- **Allow Access to Security Safes:**Sharing access to important things like safes promotes trust.
- **Involve Them in Major Decisions:**Your spouse should be part of making significant decisions in the relationship.
- **Inclusion:**Include your spouse in your life's plans and goals.

- **Ask Their Opinion:**Regularly ask your spouse how they feel about certain matters to show that you value their input.
- **Be Patient:**Understand that building trust takes time, especially if it has been broken before.
- **Be Loving:**Show your spouse that you care through your actions and words.
- **Be Understanding:**Try to see things from your spouse's perspective.
- **Show Dependability:**Be someone your spouse can rely on, no matter what.
- **Be Available:**Make time for your spouse and be present in the relationship.
- **Protect Them Emotionally:**Avoid doing things that will hurt your spouse's feelings.
- **Be Sensitive to Their Needs and Wants:**Pay attention to what your spouse needs and wants and try to fulfill those needs.

Creating a Safe and Secure Relationship

A relationship where both partners feel safe is one where trust and transparency reign. If you want your spouse to feel emotionally safe with you, it is essential to be open, honest, and sensitive to their needs. It is about creating an environment where your spouse does not have to worry about what you might be doing behind their back.

Building or rebuilding trust takes time and effort, but it is worth it for the health of your marriage. When your spouse feels safe with you, it strengthens your bond and deepens your connection, creating a solid foundation for a lasting relationship. Make it your goal to be the kind of partner who inspires trust and safety, and your marriage will thrive.

Chapter 26

Time Apart and Together

Take It Slow

On the road to recovery in your marriage rewind journey, it is crucial to move at your own pace. The duration and intensity of your healing process will vary depending on how long you and your spouse have been at odds, the nature of the separation, and the severity of the differences or offenses that caused the divide in the first place. Never allow outside influences to dictate the pace of your reconciliation or whether your marriage should continue. This is a journey for two, not three.

I have seen couples who have separated or even divorced get back together, proving that there is hope for anyone who genuinely wants to rebuild their marriage without the stress and pain of a divorce. Moving slowly might involve starting with simple texts, messages, or calls that say, "I was just thinking of you," whether you are living together or apart. It is entirely possible for people to live in the same home but be completely separated, even sleeping in different rooms and living as if they're mere roommates. Taking your time in this process allows you to see clearly what lies ahead and helps you avoid common pitfalls. It also gives you the space to be mindful of your own actions and behavior, ensuring that you don't repeat the mistakes that contributed to the dysfunction in your marriage.

Time Apart

Sometimes, it is healthy to take some time apart to regroup if necessary. This does not mean the end of your relationship, but rather a temporary break to gain perspective. Perhaps go on a girls' trip, or for the fellas, hang out with friends so you both can get a break from each other. If children are involved, come up with a plan together to decide who will be responsible for them while you are away. This break can be refreshing and can help you both come back with a clearer mind and a renewed sense of commitment.

Signs to Know if Your Marriage Will Potentially Work

1. **Bounce Back After Fights:** After big fights, you come back together like nothing happened.
2. **Easily Forgive:** You can easily forgive one another.
3. **Compassionate:** You show compassion towards each other.
4. **Willing to Sacrifice:** You are willing to sacrifice for each other.
5. **Truthful:** You are not afraid to tell each other the truth.
6. **Vulnerability:** You know how to be vulnerable with each other.
7. **Respect:** You respect each other.
8. **Hate Being Apart:** You hate to be apart and value each other's company.
9. **Mutual Support:** You support each other in your endeavors.

10. **Sense of Humor:** You share a sense of humor and can laugh together.
11. **Acceptance:** You accept each other's flaws.
12. **Shared Goals:** You have shared goals for the future.
13. **Conflict Resolution:** You have learned how to resolve conflicts maturely.
14. **Positive Interactions:** You have more positive interactions than negative ones.
15. **Shared Values:** You share the same core values.
16. **Attraction:** You remain attracted to one another.
17. **Best Friends:** You consider each other best friends.
18. **Room for Growth:** You allow room for growth and mistakes.
19. **Nonjudgmental:** You avoid being judgmental.
20. **Privacy:** You keep others out of your business and prioritize your relationship.

Marriage or being in a committed relationship is not for the faint of heart. It requires true commitment from both parties to make it work. There will be good days and bad days, but the good should outweigh the bad. Once you both learn each other's ways, likes, and dislikes, and understand how to avoid pushing each other's "explode" button, you'll discover that it is possible to live together in peace and harmony. No relationship is perfect, just as no person is perfect. Understanding this helps you to avoid judging your partner while being patient enough to allow them the room to make mistakes as they learn and grow—just like you.

Can You Live Without Your Significant Other?

This is the million-dollar question. To answer it truthfully, you need to be honest with yourself. What does it mean to be able to live without someone? What are the signs that tell you whether you can or cannot live without the person you are with?

Being able to live without the person you say you love means that, even if the relationship does not work out or if you can't fix the brokenness, you can move on in life without them. While it may be uncomfortable at first, you have the emotional and mental fortitude to continue living your life. This mindset comes from understanding that not everything in life is permanent. No matter how bad things get or how challenging life becomes, you have learned to accept what you cannot change. When change comes into your life, so do grace and mercy in abundance.

To answer the question, "Can I live without you?"—the answer might be "Yes, I can," but that does not mean you want to. However, if circumstances beyond your control force the situation, you can, by grace, be okay.

Signs That Indicate You May Find It Difficult to Live Without Someone You Love:

- **Can't Sleep:** You have trouble sleeping without them.
- **Can't Eat:** You lose your appetite.
- **Overeat:** You overeat to cope with the loss.
- **Thoughts of Suicide:** You have suicidal thoughts.
- **Thoughts of Hurting Your Partner:** You have thoughts of harming your partner.
- **Severe Depression:** You experience severe depression.
- **Can't Get Out of Bed:** You struggle to get out of bed in the morning.
- **Stop Bathing:** You neglect your personal hygiene.
- **Don't Want to Be Bothered:** You isolate yourself from others.
- **Seclusion:** You retreat into isolation.
- **Stalking:** You obsessively follow or track your partner.

- **Harassment:** You harass your partner or others involved.

These signs indicate that living without your significant other could be emotionally and mentally challenging. It is important to address these feelings, possibly with the help of a professional, to ensure that you are making the best decisions for your well-being and the health of your relationship.

In the end, understanding your own capacity to live without your partner can help you gain perspective on the depth of your connection and the importance of maintaining a healthy, balanced relationship. It is about finding strength in yourself while also valuing and nurturing the bond you share.

Chapter 27

Overcoming Pride

Let Go of the Pride

Pride is one of the most destructive forces in a marriage. It is an invisible barrier that often goes unnoticed until it is too late. But what exactly is pride? Pride is a consciousness of one's own dignity—a high and often inordinate opinion of one's own importance, merit, or superiority. This attitude can be cherished internally or displayed through one's conduct and interactions with others.

In the context of marriage, pride manifests itself in various ways, especially during conflicts. A prideful person finds it incredibly difficult to humble themselves enough to apologize, even when they know they are wrong. They are easily insulted when corrected and don't like being told what to do or that they made a mistake. This kind of pride is toxic to any relationship, but especially to a marriage.

The Dangers of Pride

Pride, left unchecked, can lead to the destruction of what could otherwise be a healthy and thriving marriage. A person's pride can bring things in their life, including their marriage, to ruin. Grace and understanding are often extended to those who approach life with a humble heart, but a prideful heart struggles to find peace and reconciliation.

If you are serious about getting your marriage back on track, it is imperative to let go of all pride. A marriage cannot survive if one or both partners are consumed by pride. Humility, on the other hand, is the key to resolution and healing. A humble person can say, "I'm sorry," even when they believe their partner is in the wrong, for the sake of peace and the relationship's well-being.

The Cost of Pride

I've seen many couples who deeply love each other go through a divorce simply because they couldn't humble themselves enough to reconcile over petty issues. In some cases, couples who divorced out of pride find themselves remarrying years later, after realizing that all they needed to do was humble themselves and communicate openly.

The financial and emotional burden of divorce is immense. When a marriage ends over something as avoidable as pride, it is a tragic loss for both parties. Swallowing pride is far cheaper—emotionally and financially—than going through the painful process of divorce with someone you still love.

The Power of Humility

Married couples will face rough patches in their relationship; you are not the first, and you certainly won't be the last. But only the strong and the humble will outlast these storms. Humility is not about admitting defeat or conceding to another's will—it is about valuing the relationship more than your own ego. It is about recognizing that in the grand scheme of things, the love you share is far more important than being right in a single argument.

If you and your spouse can stand together during the storms in your relationship, you can uphold one another and face those challenges as a united front. After all, aren't two better than one?

Moving Forward

To overcome pride in your marriage, start by acknowledging its presence. Reflect on how pride might influence your behavior and interactions with your spouse. Then, take active steps to practice humility in your daily life. This could mean being the first to apologize, listening without interrupting, or simply allowing your spouse to express their feelings without judgment.

Remember, a successful marriage is built on a foundation of love, respect, and humility. By letting go of pride, you open the door to deeper connection, understanding, and lasting happiness.

Chapter 28

Putting the Broken Pieces Back Together Again

Repairing a broken marriage starts with recognition. It is crucial to acknowledge that your marriage is struggling and that you need help before it is too late. Many people don't recognize the signs of a troubled marriage or choose to ignore them until it is too late. Ignoring small problems can lead to much bigger issues over time, making it harder to repair the relationship.

Just as we're taught to consult a physician when we experience symptoms of sickness or disease, we should take the same proactive approach with our marriages. Early detection of problems can make all the difference in saving a relationship. Identifying the warning signs early can help you put your marriage back on track before it completely derails.

Recognizing Early Warning Signs

Recognizing early signs of trouble in your marriage is key to addressing issues before they become insurmountable. Here are some signs that may indicate your marriage is in trouble and needs attention:

- **Stop Communicating:**A significant drop in communication is often one of the first signs of a troubled marriage. If you and your spouse are no longer talking openly or sharing your thoughts and feelings, it is a clear indication that something is wrong.
- **Staying Away:**If you or your spouse begin spending more time away from each other, avoiding being home, or finding excuses to be elsewhere, this can signal a desire to distance oneself from the relationship.
- **Loss of Interest in Your Spouse:**A noticeable decrease in interest in your spouse's life, activities, or well-being can be a red flag. When one partner stops caring about what the other is doing or feeling, it can indicate a lack of connection.
- **Fighting/Arguing Often:**Frequent arguments and conflicts, especially over minor issues, can suggest deeper underlying problems. It is important to address these conflicts rather than letting them fester and grow.
- **Depression:**Feelings of sadness or depression in one or both partners can sometimes be linked to marital problems. Emotional distress can be a response to unresolved issues or dissatisfaction in the relationship.
- **Stop Going Places Together:**If you and your spouse no longer spend time together or engage in activities you once enjoyed, it can indicate a growing emotional or physical distance.
- **Seeing Other People:**If one partner begins seeing other people or showing interest in others, it can signify a serious breach in the relationship's trust and fidelity.

- **Sleeping in Separate Bedrooms:**Choosing to sleep in separate bedrooms can be a sign of emotional distance or unresolved conflict. While sometimes necessary for practical reasons, it can also indicate a deeper disconnection.
- **Eating Separately:**Not sharing meals together can further contribute to feelings of separation. Mealtime is often an opportunity for connection and communication that should not be overlooked.
- **Stop Going to Family Functions Together:**Avoiding social or family gatherings as a couple can suggest discomfort with each other or an unwillingness to present a unified front.
- **Stop Having Sex and Being Intimate:**A lack of physical intimacy is often a significant indicator of marital distress. Physical connection is an important part of a healthy relationship, and its absence can signal deeper issues.
- **Lying About Whereabouts:**Dishonesty about where one has been or what one is doing can break trust and create further distance between partners. Trust is a cornerstone of any strong relationship.
- **Speak with Disrespect to Each Other:**Communication that lacks respect or kindness can be deeply damaging. Disrespectful behavior erodes trust and intimacy, making it difficult to rebuild the relationship.
- **Lack of Concern for Each Other's Health:**Not caring about each other's well-being, whether physical or emotional, shows a significant disconnection. Mutual concern is essential for a loving relationship.
- **Uncaring Attitude:**A general lack of empathy or concern for each other's feelings and needs is a clear sign that marriage needs attention.
- **Easily Aggravated About Even the Small Things:**If small, insignificant things your partner does start to annoy or aggravate you easily, it may indicate underlying frustration or resentment.

- **Weird Vibes:**An overall feeling of discomfort or unease around each other can suggest that something is amiss. Trust your instincts if you feel that the connection between you and your spouse isn't as it should be.

Act

If you recognize these signs in your relationship, it is important to seek help before things worsen. Consulting a professional marital counselor or coach at the first sign of trouble can provide valuable guidance and support. Professional help can offer new perspectives, communication tools, and strategies to address and resolve issues, helping you rebuild your relationship.

Remember, every relationship experiences challenges, but with awareness, communication, and a willingness to work through difficulties, it is possible to put the broken pieces back together again. Act early, prioritize your relationship, and invest in the health of your marriage to ensure a strong, lasting connection.

Chapter 29

I Love You, But I Don't Like You

I cannot stress enough the importance of being friends with your spouse. A happy marriage is one where the couple creates a bond of friendship, forming the foundation for a strong and lasting relationship. Friendship in marriage goes beyond romantic love; it is about genuinely enjoying each other's company, sharing common interests, and supporting one another through life's ups and downs.

However, it is not uncommon to find couples who love each other but do not like each other. This can be a significant problem for a relationship. How do couples get to a place where they love each other but do not like each other? While marriage can indeed be challenging, having a friendship with your spouse can help you both navigate the many obstacles that marriage can bring. On the other hand, if you are not friends and do not like your spouse, being married can become extremely uncomfortable and strained.

When you don't like your spouse, it often stems from a breakdown in the friendship aspect of your relationship. Certain behaviors and attitudes can erode this bond over time, making it difficult to maintain a positive and supportive partnership. Here are some common behaviors that can damage the friendship between spouses and should be avoided, especially when working on marriage recovery:

1. Always Complaining: Constant complaining can create a negative atmosphere in the relationship, making it difficult to enjoy each other's company. It can lead to feelings of frustration and resentment, which are toxic to both friendship and love.

2. Unappreciative: Failing to show appreciation for your spouse's efforts, big or small, can make them feel undervalued and taken for granted. Expressing gratitude is essential for maintaining a positive connection and showing that you value each other.

3. Being a Nagger: Nagging involves repeatedly criticizing or urging someone to do something, often in a bothersome or irritating manner. This behavior can be draining and lead to avoidance, creating distance between partners.

4. Fault Finding: Constantly pointing out your spouse's flaws or mistakes can make them feel judged and unworthy. This can erode self-esteem and damage the mutual respect needed for a healthy friendship and marriage.

5. Unloving: Showing a lack of affection or warmth can make your spouse feel unloved and unimportant. Love needs to be demonstrated through actions and words to reinforce the emotional bond.

6. Uncaring: Indifference or a lack of concern for your spouse's feelings, needs, or well-being can cause deep hurt. Caring for one another is a fundamental aspect of both friendship and marriage.

7. Non-Reciprocal: Relationships thrive on reciprocity. If one partner is constantly giving while the other is only taking, it can lead to resentment and imbalance. It is important to ensure that both partners feel supported and valued.

8. Never Compliment: Failing to acknowledge your spouse's positive qualities or achievements can lead to a lack of

motivation and diminished self-worth. Compliments and positive reinforcement are key to maintaining a loving and encouraging environment.

9. Unhelpful: Not offering assistance or support when your spouse needs it can make them feel alone and unsupported. Helping each other with daily tasks and challenges is an important part of being both friends and partners.

10. Laziness: A lack of effort in the relationship can cause it to stagnate. It is important to actively invest in your marriage by spending quality time together, communicating, and trying to keep the relationship strong.

11. Boring: Failing to engage in fun or interesting activities together can make the relationship feel dull and lifeless. Keeping things exciting and trying new experiences together can help maintain a sense of friendship and adventure.

12. Neglect: Ignoring your spouse's emotional or physical needs can lead to feelings of isolation and loneliness. It is important to prioritize each other and make time for the relationship, even amidst busy schedules.

By recognizing and avoiding these behaviors, couples can work towards rebuilding the friendship that is crucial for a healthy, happy marriage. Friendship fosters a deep connection, making it easier to navigate the challenges of marriage together. When you like and enjoy being around your spouse, you create a supportive environment where love can flourish.

Remember, a strong marriage is built not only on love but also on friendship. It is about being each other's confidants, cheerleaders, and partners in crime. By nurturing the friendship aspect of your relationship, you can strengthen your marriage and ensure it stands the test of time.

Chapter 30

Rebuilding After Mistakes

Everybody Deserves a Second Chance

You might be thinking, "I've given this person more than a second chance—I've given them a third, a fourth, and maybe even more." It is understandable to feel frustrated, especially when it seems like your efforts to forgive and move forward haven't been fully appreciated or reciprocated. But here's the thing: forgiving someone as many times as you want to be forgiven is a key to both personal peace and relational healing.

Let's be clear—this does not apply to situations involving physical abuse. Abuse is a game changer, and under no circumstances should anyone stay in an abusive situation. That's a non-negotiable boundary that must be respected for your safety and well-being.

But when it comes to other types of mistakes, everyone's tolerance levels are different. What might deeply bother one person could have little to no effect on another. For example, a wife might be okay with her husband getting inebriated and staying overnight at a friend's house, while another woman might be deeply hurt by that decision. Similarly, one husband might get upset if his wife frequently takes trips alone, whereas another might not mind at all.

Understanding Tolerance Levels

In a marriage, it is crucial to understand your partner's tolerance levels and boiling points. Knowing what triggers anger or disappointment in your spouse helps you navigate your relationship more effectively. The goal is to avoid these triggers as much as possible and to practice the art of forgiveness and proper communication.

If the offenses aren't detrimental to your marriage, consider giving your spouse a second, third, fourth, or even fifth chance—especially if you see them trying to change. Yes, it can be frustrating, but if they're genuinely trying, it is worth being patient.

What About Infidelity?

Now, I can hear some of you asking, "What if they cheated?" Infidelity is one of the most painful betrayals a person can experience, but it is important to remember that forgiveness is a personal choice. Many couples have faced infidelity and chosen to forgive, forget, and move past it. While it is painful and deeply hurtful, infidelity isn't an unforgivable sin.

The decision to repair a marriage after infidelity is deeply personal and depends on many factors, including whether the person is a repeat offender or if the infidelity was a one-time mistake. It is important to weigh these factors carefully.

If you choose to forgive and stay with the person who betrayed you, it is essential to truly forgive. Staying in the relationship without forgiveness will likely create a hostile and unhealthy environment, leading to more misery for both of you. If you know in your heart that you can't forgive, it may be best to move on and find peace outside of the relationship. Holding onto resentment will only harm you both.

The Financial Trap

One of the saddest situations is when a person feels they cannot leave a toxic relationship due to financial constraints. This feeling of being trapped can compound betrayal, leading to deep depression and frustration. Not only do you have to deal with the emotional pain of betrayal, but you also feel stuck in a situation with no escape.

Forgiveness, in this case, can be incredibly freeing—not for the person who betrayed you, but for yourself. It releases you from the heavy burden of bitterness and allows you to regain control over your emotions and your life.

Moving Forward with Forgiveness

Forgiving your spouse while still living with them can take time, and that's okay. Forgive at your own pace and take the time you need to figure out the best decisions for your relationship. Whether you choose to stay or go, make sure that your choice serves your mental and emotional well-being.

Forgiveness is not about excusing bad behavior or allowing yourself to be mistreated. It is about freeing yourself from the anger and pain that comes with holding onto resentment. By forgiving, you give yourself the chance to heal and move forward—whether that's within the marriage or beyond it. Ultimately, the path you choose should lead to peace, healing, and a better future, whatever that may look like for you.

Chapter 31

Protecting Your Marriage from Negative Influences

Ignore the Scoffers

In every marriage, there are times when the challenges seem insurmountable, and you may feel like throwing in the towel. These difficult moments can push you to your breaking point, leading you to share personal details about your marriage with others—something that can have serious repercussions down the line.

When you start sharing intimate details about your marriage with family or friends, especially during times of conflict, you open the door to judgment and criticism. Once you and your spouse reconcile, the people you have confided in may continue to harbor negative feelings toward your spouse based on the one-sided story you told them. This can create tension and resentment, not just within your marriage but also in your relationships with those who now see your spouse in a negative light.

It is important to remember that when you share your side of a story, especially in a moment of anger or hurt, you are often seeking validation and support. However, this can be unfair to your spouse and detrimental to your relationship. People who care about you might find it difficult to understand why you would stay in a relationship with someone you have spoken negatively about. This is why it is so dangerous to involve others in your marital issues.

The Importance of Keeping Marital Affairs Private

Marriage is a deeply personal relationship between two people. While it is natural to seek support during tough times, it is crucial to be mindful of what and how much you share with others. Those who love you may be quick to judge based on the information you provide, but they don't have the full picture. There are always two sides to every story, and sharing only your perspective can lead to biased opinions and advice.

I always advise people to stay out of married couples' business, even if one partner comes to them to vent. Don't judge based on a one-sided story, and don't take sides. If you are a person of faith, the best thing you can do is offer up a prayer for the couple. You never know what challenges they're facing or what will happen next—couples who fight often make up, and sometimes even divorced couples find their way back to each other and remarry.

People may laugh, mock, or scoff at your decisions, but it is essential to ignore them. Do what is best for your life, because at the end of the day, your marriage is about you and your spouse—no one else. Don't let the opinions of others keep you away from the person you love. It might feel uncomfortable or even embarrassing to remain in the relationship after sharing your grievances with others, but don't let that stop you from following your heart.

Feelings change, and so do people's hearts. Whatever challenges you are facing now, they too shall pass. Everything will be fine in time, especially if you believe that you and your spouse are meant to be together. Follow your heart, not your emotions. Emotions can be unreliable and lead you to make decisions you might regret later. Besides, no one else knows the tests your marriage is undergoing to help you both grow as individuals. How can they judge? Your marriage is your business, and no one else's.

Marriage Killers

To protect your marriage from negative influences, it is essential to be aware of the behaviors and habits that can erode your relationship. Here are some of the most common "marriage killers" to watch out for:

- **Cheating:**Infidelity is one of the most destructive forces in a marriage.
- **No Intimacy:**A lack of physical and emotional intimacy can create distance and resentment.
- **Disrespect:**Constant disrespect erodes trust and love.
- **Nagging:**Persistent nagging can lead to frustration and withdrawal.
- **Lack of Sexual Enjoyment:**An unsatisfying sex life can lead to dissatisfaction and disconnection.
- **Putting People Before Your Spouse:**Prioritizing others over your spouse can create feelings of neglect and resentment.
- **Habitual Lying:**Dishonesty destroys trust, the foundation of any relationship.
- **Lack of Communication:**Poor communication leads to misunderstandings and conflict.
- **No Trust:**Without trust, a marriage cannot thrive.
- **Unforgiveness:**Holding onto grudges can poison a relationship.
- **Holding Grudges:**Lingering resentment prevents healing and growth.

- **Laziness:**A lack of effort in the relationship can lead to dissatisfaction.
- **Not Enough Quality Time Together:**Spending time together is crucial for maintaining a strong connection.
- **Sharing Personal Business with Others:**Airing your private matters can lead to external judgment and interference.
- **Moodiness:**Uncontrolled mood swings can create an unstable environment.
- **Uncontrolled Emotions and Rage:**Unchecked emotions can lead to hurtful actions and words.
- **Not Understanding Each Other:**Misunderstanding leads to conflict and disconnect.
- **Not Listening:**Failing to listen to your spouse can make them feel unheard and unvalued.
- **Poor Hygiene:**Neglecting personal care can lead to a loss of attraction and respect.
- **Financial Irresponsibility:**Money issues are a major source of marital conflict.
- **Too Much Arguing:**Constant fighting wears down both partners and the relationship.
- **Keeping Secrets:**Secrets erode trust and intimacy.
- **Excessive Jealousy:**Jealousy can lead to controlling behavior and resentment.
- **Not Being Sensitive to Each Other's Needs:**Failing to meet each other's needs can create a rift in the relationship.
- **Joblessness:**A lack of financial contribution can create stress and resentment.
- **Staying Unattractive and Unkempt:**Neglecting your appearance can lead to a loss of attraction.
- **Speaking Negatively All the Time:**Constant negativity can create a toxic environment.
- **Habitual Complaining:**Constant complaints can drive a wedge between partners.
- **Unreliable:**Failing to follow through on commitments undermines trust.

- **Selfishness:**Putting your needs above your spouse's can lead to resentment.
- **Dishonesty:**Dishonesty creates a foundation of mistrust.
- **Sneaky Behavior:**Acting in a secretive manner fosters suspicion and doubt.
- **Work Wives or Husbands:**Inappropriate relationships at work can lead to emotional infidelity.
- **Sneaky Links:**Engaging in secretive, inappropriate relationships is a betrayal of trust.

Protecting Your Marriage

By being mindful of these marriage killers and making a conscious effort to avoid them, you can protect your relationship from negative influences. Remember, your marriage is your business, and keeping it strong requires effort, commitment, and a willingness to put each other first. Ignore the scoffers and focus on what's best for you and your spouse. Your relationship is worth the effort, and by staying united, you can overcome any challenge that comes your way.

Chapter 32

Know Them by Their Fruit

Knowing if someone truly loves you can sometimes be difficult, even if they say the words. My parents, Godfrey and Doris Martin, taught me an important lesson as a child: "Actions speak louder than words." I couldn't agree more. While some people may genuinely express their love, others might say it with ulterior motives. Before you agree to marry someone, enter a relationship, or if you are trying to determine if your current partner truly loves you, it is crucial to observe their actions over time.

Unfortunately, people can often wear masks at the beginning of a relationship to hide their true selves for various reasons. Just like a pregnancy, where the changes may not be immediately visible, the truth about someone's character and intentions will eventually become apparent with time. My mother also used to say, "Everything that's done in darkness will be brought to the light." Time reveals all things eventually, which is why it is so important to be honest from the very beginning of a relationship.

Rather than taking someone's word for their love, it is essential to know them by their fruit—to observe their actions and behaviors to truly understand their feelings and intentions. Here are some key signs to look for to determine if someone genuinely loves you:

1. Patience: A person who loves you will be patient with you, understanding that everyone has flaws and that relationships take time to grow and strengthen.
2. Kindness: Genuine love is often demonstrated through consistent acts of kindness. A loving partner shows care and compassion, not just in words but through their daily actions.
3. Supportive: Someone who truly loves you will support your dreams, ambitions, and goals. They will encourage you to be the best version of yourself and stand by you through thick and thin.
4. Sacrifice: Love often involves making sacrifices for the well-being of your partner. This could mean compromising on small things or making significant life changes to accommodate your partner's needs.
5. Honesty: A person who loves you will be honest with you, even when the truth is difficult to share. Honesty is the foundation of trust in any relationship.
6. Concern: Genuine love includes concern for your well-being —both physical and emotional. A loving partner will want to ensure you are safe, healthy, and happy.
7. Benevolent: Someone who loves you will act with generosity and goodwill. They will give of themselves freely, without expecting anything in return.
8. Vulnerable: Love requires vulnerability. A person who loves you will open up about their fears, hopes, and dreams, allowing you to see their true self.
9. Invest: Someone who truly loves you will invest time, effort, and energy into the relationship. They understand that building a strong connection requires dedication and commitment.
10. Protect: A loving partner will protect you, not just physically

but emotionally and mentally. They will stand up for you and safeguard your heart from harm.

11. Pay Attention to Your Needs: Genuine love involves paying attention to your needs and trying to meet them. A partner who loves you will be attuned to your feelings and desires.

12. Love Spending Time with You: Someone who truly loves you will cherish the time spent together, regardless of the activity. They enjoy your company and value the moments shared.

13. Faithful: Loyalty is a crucial component of love. A faithful partner will remain committed to you and your relationship, even when faced with temptations or challenges.

14. Easily Forgives: Love includes forgiveness. A person who truly loves you will be quick to forgive, understanding that everyone makes mistakes.

15. Exercise Self-Control: A loving partner will exercise self-control, especially in difficult situations. They will avoid actions or words that could harm you or the relationship.

16. Gentle: Gentleness is a sign of love. A partner who loves you will handle your heart with care, being mindful of your feelings and emotions.

17. Respect: Mutual respect is a cornerstone of any loving relationship. A partner who truly loves you will respect your boundaries, opinions, and individuality.

By paying attention to these signs, you can better understand whether someone's love for you is genuine. Actions speak louder than words and knowing someone by their fruit—by the way they behave and treat you —is a reliable way to gauge their true feelings.

Remember, love is not just about saying the right things but about consistently doing the right things. It is about showing up, being present, and committing to the relationship every day. When you observe these qualities in your partner, you can be confident in their love and the strength of your bond.

Chapter 33

Speak Life and Honesty

Speak Life

The words we speak carry immense power and energy, influencing the course of our lives and the lives of those around us. Our words can bless or curse, build up or tear down, and their impact can be felt deeply within our relationships, especially in marriage. The power of spoken words has been recognized throughout history, from the creation of the universe to the laws and customs that govern societies today.

In many traditions, the spoken word is revered for its ability to manifest reality. For example, in religious texts, it is said that the Creator spoke light into existence with the words, "Let there be light," and light appeared. This illustrates the profound impact that words can have, shaping our world and our experiences within it.

In our daily lives, we are encouraged to speak positive affirmations over ourselves and our loved ones to promote growth, healing, and positivity. Just as nurturing words can help plants grow, so can affirmational words help our marriages flourish. By consciously choosing to speak life over your marriage, you set the stage for a relationship filled with love, understanding, and success.

Affirmations, Declarations, and Decrees for Your Marriage

Recite these affirmations regularly to reinforce positivity and strength in your marriage:

I Declare and Decree

1. My marriage will survive.
2. My marriage is blessed.
3. No weapon formed against us, naturally or spiritually, will prosper.
4. Let us have no successful enemies.
5. Let everything intended for our demise be turned around for our good.
6. We are a successful couple.
7. We live in peace and harmony with each other.
8. We understand and respect one another.
9. Our children are blessed.
10. Our entire family is blessed.
11. We love and walk in total forgiveness towards each other.
12. We are financially blessed.
13. We live debt-free lives.
14. We live in grace and mercy.
15. Let no good thing be withheld from us.
16. Let our enemies be at peace with us.
17. Let my family be fully protected from all harm.
18. I speak life over my marriage.
19. We only have eyes for each other.
20. Let there be no betrayal of any kind among us.

21. We trust each other.
22. Let us both be totally healed and made whole.
23. I speak total healing and restoration over me and my spouse.
24. Let us not know lack.
25. For our shame, let us have double.
26. Let us rise above all negative circumstances and situations.
27. Let every negative word spoken against us through family, friends, or foes be sent back to where it originated.
28. Let the spirit of jealousy be pushed back.
29. Let goodness and mercy follow us all the days of our lives.
30. May we both walk in divine purpose.

Honesty Is the Best Policy

The foundation of any strong and healthy marriage is built on trust, and trust is maintained through honesty. Being truthful with your spouse, even when it is uncomfortable or embarrassing, is crucial for the longevity of your relationship. When you lie about even the smallest things, it creates a tear in the fabric of your relationship—a tear that can widen with each subsequent lie or act of dishonesty until it eventually leads to a breakdown of trust and connection.

Secrets and omissions are forms of dishonesty that can be just as damaging as outright lies. When the truth eventually comes to light, as it often does, the impact can be devastating. This is why it is essential to practice honesty at all costs, even when you fear the consequences.

Fear is often the root cause of dishonesty. You might fear your spouse's reaction or the potential fallout from the truth, but maintaining integrity in your relationship is far more important. When you choose honesty, you build a foundation of trust that can withstand challenges and conflicts.

Practicing Honesty in Your Marriage

1. **Be Transparent:**Share your true feelings, thoughts, and experiences with your spouse. Don't withhold information that you know they would want to know.
2. **Address Fears:**Understand that if you feel the need to lie, it is likely because of fear. Confront this fear by being open and honest, which will strengthen your relationship in the long run.
3. **Start with the Truth:**Never enter a relationship with lies about who you are or what you have been through. Begin with honesty to build a strong foundation.
4. **Avoid Secrets:**Even if you think a secret is small or insignificant, it can still erode trust. Practice full transparency with your spouse.
5. **Make Honesty a Habit:**Consistently practice honesty in all aspects of your relationship. This will create a culture of trust and openness, which is essential for a healthy marriage.
6. **Understand the Consequences of Dishonesty:**Recognize that dishonesty, even in small matters, can have significant consequences. It is not worth risking the trust you have built with your spouse.

By committing to honesty and speaking life into your marriage, you create an environment where love, trust, and mutual respect can thrive. These principles are the bedrock of a strong, resilient marriage that can weather any storm.

Chapter 34

Spice Is Nice

Adding some spice is nice in any relationship. A common concern I hear from couples is that their spouse has become boring in the bedroom or makes little to no effort to initiate romance. After listening to several couples, I've concluded that this is a real issue that needs to be addressed to maintain a healthy and satisfying relationship. It is important for couples not to take each other for granted and to openly communicate their desires and needs.

Being able to express your sexual needs and desires to your partner without fear or hesitation is essential. Likewise, being receptive and willing to accommodate each other's desires can strengthen the bond and enhance intimacy. Mutual satisfaction in a relationship is not just about physical pleasure; it is also about feeling valued, understood, and cherished by your partner.

Keeping Up Appearances

One aspect of keeping the romance alive is maintaining your appearance for each other. It is easy to become complacent over time, but effort in this area can make a significant difference. Ladies, it is important to keep your appearance up, especially during romantic encounters. Avoid wearing hair bonnet or old, raggedy night clothes when you are trying to create a romantic atmosphere. Instead, choose something that makes you feel confident and attractive. Similarly, men should also try to look and smell good for their partners. Women appreciate a well-groomed, good-smelling man who shows he cares about his appearance.

Regardless of how long you have been married—whether it is 5, 10, 15, or even 25 years—continuing to put effort into your appearance can keep the spark alive. The same things you did to attract your spouse initially should be maintained throughout your marriage to keep that attraction strong.

Understanding Life Changes

It is also important to acknowledge that life can sometimes take a toll on our desire for intimacy. Traumatic events, stress, and other life challenges can reduce the desire to be romantic, and this is completely understandable. Women go through many changes as they age—hormonally, physically, psychologically, and emotionally—that can impact their libido. During these times, patience, love, and friendship are crucial in supporting your partner as they navigate these changes.

Men also face their own set of challenges that can affect their desire for romance, from stress to physical health issues. For those experiencing physical, hormonal, emotional, or mental challenges, the focus should be on healing and support rather than pressure to be romantic. However, for those who are physically and emotionally capable, there is no excuse not to try to spice up your love life for the sake of your marriage.

Understanding Your Partner's Preferences

What's spicy for one person may be different for another. For example, my husband loves to see me in a natural, slightly undone state—when my nightgown is casually falling off my shoulders and my hair is naturally tousled, with no makeup. Sometimes, men prefer a more natural look over makeup and elaborate outfits. Understanding your partner's preferences and desires is key to keeping intimacy alive.

It is important to know and discuss any sexual boundaries you and your partner may have. Open communication about what you enjoy and what makes you feel comfortable can help ensure that both partners are satisfied and fulfilled. Whether your partner is into fishnet stockings and high heels or prefers a softer, more natural approach, it is about finding what works for both of you and embracing it.

For those who have sexual insecurities or body image concerns, it can be helpful to talk to a professional. A therapist or sex coach can provide guidance and support to help you, or your partner overcome these insecurities and fully enjoy your intimate relationship. If your partner has insecurities, be patient and loving. Avoid making them feel bad about their feelings and support them in seeking the help they need.

Ways to Spice Up Your Relationship

Here are a few things you and your partner can try to add some spice to your relationship:

- **Dressing Sexy:** Wear outfits that make you feel confident and desirable.

- **Lighting Romantic Candles:**Create a sensual atmosphere with soft lighting and fragrant candles.
- **Love Music:**Play romantic music to set the mood.
- **Slow Gentle Sensual Touches and Kisses Naked:**Take your time exploring each other's bodies with slow, gentle touches and kisses.
- **Role Playing:**Introduce some playful role-playing to add excitement and variety.
- **Book a Romantic Getaway:**Take a break from everyday life and enjoy a romantic getaway together.
- **Try Different Sex Positions:**Experiment with new positions to keep things interesting.
- **Play a Sex-Related Game:**Explore each other's fantasies and desires with fun, adult games.
- **Start Sexting While Away from Each Other:**Build anticipation and excitement by sending flirty messages.
- **Share with Each Other Your Sexual Fantasies:**Be open about your fantasies and explore them together.
- **Explore Each Other:**Spend time exploring each other's likes and dislikes in a non-judgmental way.
- **Be Spontaneous:**Surprise your partner with unexpected romantic gestures.
- **Understand & Speak Each Other's Love Language:**Learn and practice each other's love languages to deepen your emotional connection.
- **Surprise Gifts Just Because:**Give thoughtful gifts that show you are thinking of your partner.
- **Hire a Sex Coach:**Consider hiring a sex coach to help improve your intimacy and sexual satisfaction.
- **Have a Romantic Dinner:**Cook or order a special meal and enjoy a candlelit dinner at home.
- **Change Up Your Look, Try Something New:**Keep things fresh by trying out new styles or looks that appeal to your partner.

Keeping romance alive in a marriage requires effort, creativity, and a willingness to explore new things together. By communicating openly, understanding each other's desires, and trying to keep things exciting, couples can maintain a strong and passionate connection for years to come.

Chapter 35

Benefits of Marriage

Marriage can offer numerous benefits that span across financial, legal, and emotional aspects of life. These benefits can contribute to a more stable, secure, and fulfilling partnership.

Emotional Benefits

Marriage can also provide substantial emotional benefits that contribute to overall well-being:

- Stronger Support System: Being married often means having a reliable and consistent support system. This emotional support can help alleviate stress, provide a sense of security, and contribute to better mental health.
- Stability and Companionship: A healthy marriage offers stability and companionship, which can enhance life satisfaction and overall happiness. Knowing that you have a partner to share life's ups and downs with can be incredibly comforting and fulfilling.

Financial Benefits

Marriage can enhance financial stability for several reasons:

- Dual Incomes: Married couples often have two sources of income, which can lead to greater financial stability compared to unmarried or single individuals. This can make it easier to manage household expenses, save for the future, and achieve financial goals.
- Health Insurance Plans: Many married couples have access to family health insurance plans that offer discounts for covering the entire family. This can result in significant savings on healthcare costs.
- Lower Insurance Claims: Statistics have shown that married couples tend to file fewer insurance claims than single people. This can lead to lower insurance premiums and additional savings.

Legal Benefits

Marriage also comes with a variety of legal benefits, which can provide protection and rights for both partners:

- Employment Benefits: Married couples may be eligible for a range of employment benefits, such as health insurance coverage, family leave, and bereavement leave, which may not be available to unmarried partners.
- Family Benefits: Marriage grants certain family rights, such as adoption rights and joint foster care rights, making it easier for couples to start or expand their family together.
- Government Benefits: Spouses are often entitled to receive government benefits after their partner's death, such as Social

Security benefits, disability benefits, and Veterans Affairs (VA) benefits.

- Tax and Estate Planning Benefits: Married couples enjoy various tax advantages, including the ability to transfer an unlimited amount of assets to each other without incurring gift or estate taxes. Additionally, money left to a spouse is typically not subject to federal estate tax, providing further financial protection.

Other Benefits of Marriage

Beyond the core financial, legal, and emotional advantages, marriage offers additional benefits, including:

1. IRA Benefits: Spouses can contribute to each other's Individual Retirement Accounts (IRAs), potentially increasing their retirement savings.
2. Insurance Plans: Married couples often receive better rates on various types of insurance, including health, life, and auto insurance.
3. Social Security: Married individuals may be eligible for spousal Social Security benefits, which can increase their retirement income.
4. Employment Benefits: Spouses can benefit from each other's employment benefits, such as health insurance and retirement plans.
5. Inheritance Benefits: Marriage can simplify inheritance processes, often ensuring that assets pass smoothly to the surviving spouse.
6. Health Leave: Married couples are often entitled to take leave to care for a sick spouse, which may not be an option for unmarried partners.

7. Tax Breaks: Married couples can benefit from various tax breaks, including the ability to file jointly, which can lead to a lower overall tax burden.
8. Gift Taxes: Spouses can transfer unlimited amounts of money and property to each other without incurring gift taxes.
9. Estate Taxes: Spouses can inherit an unlimited amount of assets from each other without facing federal estate taxes.
10. Lower Tax Bracket: Filing jointly can sometimes result in a lower tax bracket, reducing the overall tax burden for the couple.
11. Estate Protection: Marriage can provide additional legal protections for an estate, ensuring that a surviving spouse receives the assets.
12. Life Insurance Plans: Married couples may have access to better life insurance plans and rates, providing financial security for the surviving spouse.
13. Veterans' Benefits: Spouses of veterans may be eligible for various benefits, including healthcare, education, and survivor benefits.

Marriage offers a wide range of benefits that can enhance financial stability, provide legal protections, and improve emotional well-being. These advantages make marriage a meaningful commitment that goes beyond love, contributing to a secure and supportive partnership.

Chapter 36

Financial Oneness

Love and Money

The concept of oneness in marriage extends beyond emotional and spiritual connection; it also encompasses financial unity. Money, or rather the mismanagement and misunderstanding of it, is one of the leading causes of stress and divorce in marriages. Understanding the power of financial oneness can be transformative for a relationship, turning a potential source of conflict into an area of strength.

When financial hardships arise, it is important for both partners to come together, pooling their resources to ensure the stability and security of the household. This collective approach not only alleviates stress but also reinforces the bond between you and your spouse. In a loving marriage, there should be nothing you wouldn't do for each other, including supporting one another through financial difficulties.

The Power of Shared Finances

Bringing your financial resources together can have a profoundly positive impact on your relationship. It is a tangible expression of the trust and commitment you share. While some couples choose to maintain separate bank accounts, which can work perfectly fine, having a shared account can enhance trust and communication. A joint account requires both partners to be accountable to each other for their spending, fostering a sense of partnership and responsibility.

When both partners contribute to and manage a shared account, it opens the door to greater transparency in the relationship. It encourages open communication about financial decisions and ensures that both of you are on the same page when it comes to managing household expenses. This kind of financial unity can prevent misunderstandings and conflicts that might otherwise arise from separate, undisclosed spending habits.

Building Trust and Communication Through Financial Oneness

Operating from a shared account necessitates a high level of communication. Each partner needs to inform the other about their expenditures to maintain a balanced account and avoid overdrafts. This practice not only helps in keeping the finances in order but also builds trust, as both partners must be honest and transparent about their spending.

Furthermore, managing money together reinforces the idea that you are a team—working towards common goals and supporting each other in the process. It teaches you how to collaborate effectively, making decisions together that benefit the entire household. By learning to manage your finances as a unit, you strengthen the foundation of your marriage.

The Benefits of Financial Unity

When you and your spouse achieve financial oneness, several positive outcomes can follow:

- **Increased Trust:**Sharing finances requires trust and honesty, which strengthens your relationship.
- **Enhanced Communication:**Regular discussions about money foster better communication skills that can translate into other areas of your marriage.
- **Accountability:**Being accountable to each other for your spending helps prevent financial mismanagement and builds mutual respect.
- **Teamwork:**Working together towards financial stability reinforces the idea that you are partners in every aspect of life, not just emotionally but practically as well.
- **Security:**A shared approach to finances can provide a greater sense of security and stability, knowing that you are both committed to the financial well-being of your family.

By embracing financial oneness, you create a more unified and harmonious relationship. It is not just about combining resources; it is about combining lives in a way that reflects your mutual love, trust, and commitment. This financial unity can serve as a strong pillar in your marriage, helping you navigate the inevitable ups and downs with confidence and solidarity.

Chapter 37

The Does and Don'ts of a Healthy Marriage

The Dos and Don'ts

Dos

1. **Honesty is the Best Policy:** Always be truthful with each other, even when it is uncomfortable. Trust is built on a foundation of honesty.
2. **Compliment and Affirm:** Your spouse should hear more compliments from you than from anyone else. Fill each other's lives with positive words.
3. **Stay Positive:** Cultivate a positive atmosphere in your home. Your attitude sets the tone for your relationship.
4. **Take Time Away from Others:** Focus on your relationship by pulling back from others for a while. Spend about a month dedicated to each other, and people will understand.
5. **Forgive Quickly:** Allow yourselves to make mistakes and be quick to forgive. Holding onto grudges only damages your relationship.
6. **Wine and Dine:** Regularly take time to enjoy each other's company. Date nights and special outings can rekindle your romance.

7. **Sleep Naked Together and Cuddle:**Physical closeness builds emotional intimacy. Cuddling can help you bond and feel more connected.

8. **Be Vulnerable:**Open-up to one another. Vulnerability strengthens trust and deepens your connection.

9. **Seek Marital Counseling:**Counseling is a great tool to help you navigate challenges and grow stronger together.

10. **Stay Open and Transparent:**Be open about your feelings, thoughts, and experiences. Transparency prevents misunderstandings and builds trust.

11. **Double Date with Positive Married Friends:**Spend time with other couples who have a positive influence on your marriage.

12. **Pray Together:**Praying together can strengthen your spiritual connection and provide comfort during tough times.

13. **Rekindle Simple Activities:**Start doing simple things together, like taking a walk in the park while holding hands. These small gestures help remove emotional distance and rebuild your bond.

14. **Watch Your Tone:**Speak respectfully to each other, even during disagreements. Your spouse is your partner, not your child, and deserves to be spoken to with kindness and consideration.

15. **Say Good Morning and Good Night:**These simple greetings set a positive tone for the day and help you end on a good note.

16. **Morning Hugs:**A morning hug is a great way to start the day with love and connection.

17. **Send Loving Texts:**Whether you are at work or in the next room, sending loving messages throughout the day creates a fun and affectionate atmosphere.

18. **Give Just-Because Gifts:**Surprise your spouse with small, affordable gifts "just because." These gestures show that you are thinking of them and can brighten their day.

19. **Tell Your Spouse You Love Them:**Even if you have been fighting, saying "I love you" can help in the healing process. Your heart will follow your words, helping to rebuild your connection.

20. **Make Each Other Feel Safe:**Understand what makes your spouse feel safe and secure and make those things a priority in your relationship.

21. **Express Your Need for Each Other:**Tell your spouse how much you need and appreciate them. This reinforces your bond and shows that you value their presence in your life.

22. **Create a Positive Atmosphere:**What you do and say shapes the atmosphere in your home. Aim to create an environment of love, peace, and understanding.

Don'ts

1. **Don't Start New Relationships While Married:**If you are angry or separated, starting a new relationship can complicate things if you decide to work things out. It creates unnecessary emotional baggage and trust issues.

2. **Don't Engage in Unnecessary Fights:**Avoid conflicts that don't contribute to resolving issues. Some battles aren't worth fighting and can create more harm than good.

3. **Don't Allow Others to Speak Negatively About Your Spouse:**Protect your relationship from outside negativity. People's opinions can influence how you view your spouse and your marriage.

4. **Don't Mention Divorce Lightly:**Saying "I want a divorce" in the heat of an argument can plant seeds of doubt in both your minds. Words have power; be careful not to say something you don't truly mean.

5. **Don't Disconnect from Your Spouse:**No matter the circumstances, maintain your connection. Emotional and physical distance can grow quickly if left unchecked.

6. **Don't Allow Invitations That Exclude Your Spouse:** Attending events where your spouse is not welcome can cause tension. If your spouse has issues with your family or friends, work towards reconciliation to maintain harmony in your relationship.

By following these dos and avoiding the don'ts, you can create a strong, healthy marriage that withstands the challenges of life. These practices help maintain connection, trust, and love in your relationship, ensuring that you and your spouse continue to grow together in harmony and mutual respect.

Chapter 38

Revisiting and Strengthening Your Marriage

Rehearsing the Past

Revisiting the past can be detrimental to the healing and recovery of your marriage. Continuously reminding your partner of past offenses only serves to keep you both stuck in a cycle of pain and resentment. This behavior prevents the necessary space for healing, deepens the wounds, and creates further disconnection. To move forward and grow, both partners need to consciously decide to let go of the past.

Holding on to negative memories keeps you in a vicious cycle of resentment, which hinders your ability to forgive and move on. It is crucial to make a deliberate choice to release these painful thoughts. Every time a hurtful memory surfaces, consciously reject it and replace it with something positive that brings you joy. This process requires time, practice, and patience, but it is essential for your mental and emotional well-being. Taking control of your thoughts and choosing to focus on positive, uplifting things will help you break free from the grip of past hurts.

Marriage Rewind Tips

Rewinding your marriage to a place of peace and love requires intentional effort and commitment. Here are some tips to help you reconnect and strengthen your bond:

1. **Stop Everything:** Pause and take a step back from your usual routine to focus solely on your relationship.
2. **Pull Back from Everyone:** Distance yourselves from outside influences and prioritize your time together.
3. **Plan Private Time Alone:** Set aside a week or more for just the two of you. Put your phone on "Do Not Disturb" to avoid distractions.
4. **Discuss Softly and Respectfully:** Talk about what led you to this point without placing blame. Take accountability for your actions.
5. **Repent, Apologize, and Forgive:** Sincerely apologize for any wrongs, seek forgiveness, and extend forgiveness to your partner.
6. **Embrace Each Other:** Physical closeness, including good sex, can help re-establish intimacy.
7. **Unplug Together:** Spend time in bed without TV or devices, focusing on each other.
8. **Start the Re-bonding Process:** Sleep naked while holding each other to feel the physical and emotional connection.
9. **Non-Sexual Touch:** Hold and touch each other in a comforting, non-sexual way to strengthen your bond.
10. **Romantic Dinners:** Share meals together, whether at home or in a restaurant, to enjoy each other's company.
11. **Stay Away from Others:** Use this time to focus solely on your relationship without outside interference.
12. **Speak Kindly:** During this period, only say positive things to each other to rebuild trust and affection.
13. **Avoid Serious Conversations:** After your initial discussion,

steer clear of negative or heavy topics, especially those that might bring up the past.

14. **Remind Each Other of the Positives:**Talk about the qualities that made you fall in love with each other.
15. **Go on a Date:**After a few days of reconnecting, plan a date that you both enjoy.
16. **Take Showers Together:**If possible, shower together to increase intimacy and bonding.
17. **Plan a Vow Renewal:**Consider renewing your vows to reaffirm your commitment to each other.
18. **Inform Others of Your Efforts:**Let those you previously talked about a possible divorce know that you are working on your marriage. Ask for their support in forgiving your spouse and giving you space to heal.
19. **Let Go of Negativity:**Get rid of anything that reminds you of past conflicts, including photos, documents, messages, or inappropriate relationships.
20. **Pray Together:**If you are a person of faith, pray together to seek guidance and strength in your relationship.

Bonding is crucial for any relationship, and it is the little things that make a big difference. Even if you can't afford extravagant gestures, simple, heartfelt actions—like creating a romantic space with candles and music in your home—can make a significant impact. The most important thing is that you are together, working towards a stronger, healthier marriage.

Tips for Reconnection

Reconnecting with your spouse requires consistency, presence, and shared experiences. Here are some tips to help you reconnect:

- **Spend Quality Uninterrupted Time Together:**Make time for each other without interruptions or distractions.

- **Eliminate Distractions:**Turn off the TV, put away your phones, and focus on each other.
- **Prioritize Your Alone Time:**Ensure that your time together is a priority in your daily routine.
- **Be Consistent:**Regularly spend time together and make it a non-negotiable part of your relationship.
- **Be Completely Present Mentally:**Engage fully with your spouse during your time together, both mentally and emotionally.
- **Find Activities You Both Enjoy:**Whether it is exercising, taking trips, reading books, playing board games, or hiking, find activities that you can do together to strengthen your bond.

Revisiting and strengthening your marriage is a process that requires effort, patience, and a commitment to growth. By focusing on the present and working together to build a strong foundation, you can create a fulfilling and lasting relationship.

Examples of Small Bonding Practices

1. **Body Massages:**Giving each other body massages can be a relaxing way to connect physically and emotionally. It helps reduce stress and promotes physical touch, which is crucial for building intimacy in a relationship.
2. **Foot Rubs:**A simple gesture like rubbing your partner's feet can provide comfort and show affection. It is a nurturing act that conveys care and attention to your partner's well-being.
3. **Scalp Rubs:**A soothing scalp rub can be incredibly relaxing and is another form of gentle, intimate touch that can bring partners closer together. It is a simple way to show affection and care.

4. **Laying Naked Together:**Physical closeness and vulnerability are essential for intimacy. Laying naked together allows couples to feel comfortable with each other's bodies and promotes a sense of trust and openness.

5. **Feeding Each Other:**Feeding each other, whether it is a piece of fruit or a special dessert, is a playful and intimate act that encourages closeness. It is a small, romantic gesture that can make mealtimes more enjoyable.

6. **Going Walking:**Taking a walk together offers time for conversation and connection away from the distractions of daily life. It allows couples to enjoy each other's company in a relaxed setting.

7. **Going to the Movies (Date Nights):**Date nights, like going to the movies, provide a break from routine and an opportunity to spend quality time together. It is a chance to create shared experiences and memories.

8. **Sitting in a Park While Holding Hands:**Simply sitting in a park and holding hands can be a peaceful way to bond. It is a quiet moment of connection that allows couples to enjoy each other's presence without needing to talk.

9. **Shoulder Rubs:**A gentle shoulder rub can relieve tension and show support. It is a comforting touch that demonstrates love and care, especially after a long day.

10. **Holding Hands While Driving or Lying in Bed:**Holding hands, whether while driving or lying in bed, is a simple yet powerful way to stay connected. It symbolizes unity and affection in everyday moments.

11. **Cooking Together:**Preparing a meal together can be a fun and collaborative activity that brings couples closer. It encourages teamwork and provides a sense of accomplishment when you enjoy the meal you have created together.

12. **Cleaning Together:**Working together on household chores can be a bonding experience. It fosters cooperation and shows

that both partners are willing to contribute to maintaining their shared space.

13. **Working on Small Projects Together:**Whether it is a DIY project or gardening, working on a project together helps strengthen your partnership. It is a way to achieve something together and enjoy the process.

14. **Playing Games Together:**Playing board games, card games, or even video games together can be a fun way to unwind and connect. It encourages friendly competition and laughter, strengthening your bond.

15. **Going on Trips Together:**Traveling together, even for a short trip, creates lasting memories and allows you to explore new places and experiences as a couple. It is a great way to build shared history and adventure.

16. **Kissing:**Regular kisses, whether quick pecks or longer, more passionate kisses, are a vital part of maintaining intimacy and affection in a relationship. It is a simple yet powerful way to express love.

17. **Pillow Fighting:**A playful pillow fight can be a lighthearted way to have fun and engage in physical activity together. It encourages laughter and spontaneity, which are great for bonding.

18. **Talking Trash About Each Other in a Fun-Loving Way (Cracking Jokes):**Playfully teasing each other can be a fun way to show affection and lighten the mood. It is important that this is done in a loving, respectful manner that both partners enjoy.

19. **Crack Jokes About Other People Together (Nothing Serious or Damaging):**Sharing a laugh over harmless jokes can create a sense of camaraderie and shared humor. It is a way to enjoy each other's company and relax together.

20. **Discover a Favorite Song Just for You Both:**Finding a song that you both love can become a special part of your relationship. It is a shared treasure that can evoke happy memories whenever you hear it.

21. **Work Out Together:**Exercising as a couple can be a motivating and bonding experience. It is a way to support each other's health goals while spending time together.

22. **Read Together:**Whether you are reading the same book or sharing passages from different ones, reading together can be a quiet and intimate way to connect. It encourages discussion and deepens your intellectual bond.

23. **Sing Together at Home or in the Car (Make Fun Videos):**Singing together, especially in a relaxed setting like at home or in the car, can be a joyful way to connect. Making fun videos can add an extra layer of playfulness and create lasting memories.

24. **Take Up for Each Other (You Mess with My Spouse, You Mess with Me):**Defending and supporting each other in public or private shows loyalty and strengthens the bond between you. It reinforces the idea that your area team and always have each other's back.

25. **Outdoor Nature Hikes or Camping (Fun Outdoor Activities):**Spending time in nature together, whether hiking, camping, or enjoying other outdoor activities, is a great way to disconnect from the daily grind and reconnect with each other. It fosters a sense of adventure and exploration as a couple.

26. **Praying Together:**For couples who share a faith, praying together can be a deeply spiritual and unifying practice. It reinforces a shared belief system and helps build a strong foundation of faith in your relationship.

Engaging in these small bonding practices helps couples maintain intimacy, connection, and fun in their relationship. These activities encourage spending quality time together and nurturing the love and affection that keeps a relationship strong and healthy.

Chapter 39

Final Commitment

You are Mine and I am Yours-That's All to It

In marriage, it is not uncommon for couples to occasionally wonder if there might have been someone else out there, someone who might have been a better fit. Especially during difficult times, when you and your spouse aren't seeing eye to eye, these thoughts can creep in, leading you to question your choice. You might think about the possibilities— what if you had waited, what if there was someone else who was better looking, more successful, more attentive, or who simply seemed more compatible?

But here's the truth: there will always be someone out there who might seem like a better option on the surface. Someone who appears to have qualities that your spouse may lack. However, entertaining these thoughts is a dangerous game. It plants seeds of doubt and discontent in your mind, which can slowly erode the foundation of your marriage.

When you said your vows, you entered a covenant—a solemn agreement between two people who promise to love, honor, and cherish each other. This covenant is not to be taken lightly. Allowing your mind to wander into the realm of "what if" only opens the door to disloyalty and undermines the commitment you have made.

Yes, it is possible that there's someone out there who might have different or even "better" qualities than your spouse, but it is important to remember that everyone comes with their own set of challenges and imperfections. The grass isn't always greener on the other side. No one is perfect, including you. Just as you might think you could find someone better, so could your spouse. The key is to stop focusing on what you think might be out there and instead pour your energy into cultivating what you already have.

Think of your spouse as a garden that you have inherited, full of potential but also in need of care. There may be weeds that need pulling (flaws or habits that need addressing), but with nurturing, love, and attention, you can help your spouse—and your marriage—flourish. Speak positive words, encourage them in their strengths, and support them in their growth. The more you invest in your marriage, the more rewarding the relationship will be.

Until Death Do Us Part

"Until death do us part." These words, often spoken at the end of wedding vows, signify a lifelong commitment—a promise to stay together until one of you passes away. While this is typically understood to refer to physical death, it is important to consider another perspective: the death of a marriage through divorce.

Death, in a broader sense, can mean the end or destruction of something. Just as physical death ends a person's life, divorce ends a marriage. Both are deeply painful and signify the permanent separation of two beings who were once united.

Divorce is often described as a painful process, akin to a death, because it involves the tearing apart of lives that were once intertwined. It is not just the legal dissolution of a marriage; it is the emotional and spiritual severing of a bond that was meant to last a lifetime. Just as there are many causes of physical death, there are many issues that can lead to the "death" of a marriage—infidelity, lack of communication, financial stress, and growing apart, to name a few.

However, just as some physical ailments can be treated and healed, many of the issues that threaten to end a marriage can also be addressed and overcome. The choice is yours: do you allow your marriage to die, or do you fight to keep it alive? It is important to understand that you have the power to choose the outcome of your marriage. If you and your spouse are willing to work together, to confront the challenges head-on and recommit to each other, your marriage can survive and even thrive.

A marriage does not have to end in divorce. With effort, communication, and mutual respect, you can keep your marriage alive and strong. The commitment you made on your wedding day wasn't just for the good times—it was for the challenging times as well. By choosing to honor that commitment, you can build a marriage that withstands the tests of time and grows stronger with each passing year.

Chapter 40

Your Assignment

Your Assignment

A thriving marriage requires consistent nurturing, love, and attention. One of the simplest yet most powerful ways to maintain and strengthen your connection with your spouse is through daily affirmations and gestures that plant and water positive seeds in their heart. These small, intentional acts of love and appreciation can create a strong foundation for a lasting and fulfilling relationship.

Here are some things you can say or do daily to help cultivate positivity in your marriage:

- **"I love you"**:This simple phrase, when said sincerely, reaffirms your commitment and affection.
- **"You are simply amazing"**:Acknowledge the qualities that make your spouse unique and special.
- **"I appreciate all that you do"**:Show gratitude for their efforts, whether big or small, and let them know their contributions don't go unnoticed.
- **"You are so beautiful/handsome"**:Compliment your

spouse's appearance to boost their confidence and remind them of your attraction.

- **"You are all I need":**Express that they fulfill you emotionally and romantically, reinforcing your bond.
- **"I not only want you, I need you":**Convey the importance of their presence in your life.
- **"I don't know what I would do without you":**Highlight how integral they are to your happiness and well-being.
- **"I am so glad you came into my life":**Reflect on how much your spouse has enriched your life and express your gratitude for them.
- **"No one can do this like you":**Recognize their unique talents and skills, making them feel valued and indispensable.
- **"I miss you":**Let them know they are on your mind, even when you are apart.
- **"I love the way you do [this or that]":**Be specific about what you admire, whether it is how they cook, their work ethic, or how they handle challenges.
- **Compliment Their Appearance:**Praise their hair, clothing, makeup, scent, or anything that stands out. This helps them feel seen and appreciated.
- **Support Their Efforts:**Whether they're tackling a big project or a small task, offer encouragement and let them know you are proud of their accomplishments.
- **Smile at Your Spouse:**A smile is a powerful, non-verbal expression of love, acceptance, and comfort. It can convey warmth and positivity without a single word.
- **Send an "I Love You" Text:**A quick text with a loving message or a playful, sexy emoji can brighten their day and keep the connection strong.
- **Surprise Lunch Date:**If possible, meet your spouse for a spontaneous lunch. This break from routine can be a refreshing way to reconnect—just make sure it is with your spouse, not a "sneaky link."

- **Just Because Gift:**Surprise your spouse with a small gift that says, "I was thinking of you." It does not have to be expensive—it is the thought that counts.
- **Spontaneous Getaways:**Plan a quick escape, whether it is a local adventure or a short trip out of town. These moments away from everyday life can rejuvenate your relationship.

Your assignment is to incorporate these daily actions into your routine, making them a natural part of your marriage. By doing so, you'll be continuously investing in the health and happiness of your relationship, creating a positive and loving atmosphere that allows both of you to thrive together.

Chapter 41

Prayer

Marriage Rewind Prayer for Couples

Heavenly Father, we come before You, asking for Your forgiveness for our shortcomings as we forgive each other. We acknowledge our imperfections, but we are willing to change our negative behaviors to strengthen our marriage and grow as individuals. We seek Your guidance on this journey of reconciliation, asking You to heal our hearts and minds from past and present traumas. Renew the passion and love we once had for each other and teach us how to love in the right way.

Help us to prioritize each other, not allowing any person or situation to come between us. Grant us the wisdom to maintain healthy boundaries, effective communication, friendship, loyalty, respect, kindness, patience, and sensitivity toward one another. We thank You for helping us resolve our conflicts peacefully and respectfully.

Lord, let us be sources of encouragement, strength, and support to each other, avoiding any words or actions that could tear us down. Help us to understand and fulfill our purpose for being together. Protect us from temptation, and let Your grace and mercy continue to cover us and our family now and forever. Amen.

Chapter 42

You Have the Victory

Now that you have weathered the storm and are working on rebuilding your relationship, it is essential to stand together in unity and oneness to create a strong, resilient marriage. This is the time to reflect on what went wrong, discard what is no longer useful, and begin to piece back together what was broken. There is something profoundly sacred about a couple who finds peace and togetherness after enduring challenges.

Through this journey, you will discover that all the difficulties you faced together have led you to a deeper understanding. You will realize that it is far better to lay down your pride, insecurities, and other issues and embrace peace with each other. You'll see that you are not enemies but two people who desire love, acceptance, and to be treated with kindness and respect.

You will learn that you both have unique gifts, talents, and minds that must be blended harmoniously to become one. This process can be daunting, but the rewards are immense. You will emerge as a couple who move as one, share the same vision, and work together towards common goals. You will embody the true spirit of unity and oneness, walking in divine purpose together.

Not every couple reaches this level of harmony because the journey can be challenging and filled with trials. But if you can outlast the storms, you will become an example of what a strong, enduring marriage looks like. In a world where divorce is often the first solution, your perseverance will be a testament to the power of commitment and love.

The process of self-development, learning how to treat one another, handling criticism without taking offense, forgiving and letting go, and practicing patience and understanding—all of these are part of the journey. When you have overcome the obstacles designed to hinder your progress—whether they were your own inconsistencies, pride, or selfishness—you will be ready to achieve great things together.

You have the victory together. Don't give up on each other now. After all you have been through, you owe it to yourselves to reap the harvest of your hard work and enjoy the fruits of your labor. You deserve it!

Chapter 43

No Guarantees

This book was written to help couples who genuinely want to work on and improve their relationship. However, it is important to remember that healing a relationship requires both partners to be willing participants. If your spouse isn't interested in putting in the effort to work things out, don't take it personally. People have the freedom to make their own choices, and sometimes they may decide that the relationship is no longer right for them.

It is okay if your partner does not want to stay for the long haul. Life can be unpredictable, and sometimes we face challenges that are beyond our control. Remember that you are an amazing person, and with time, you may meet someone who is the perfect match for you if that is your desire. Meanwhile, continue your path of self-healing and self-improvement, not just for the sake of a future relationship but for your own well-being and happiness.

My hope and prayer for everyone who reads this book is that you find a happy, healthy, and fulfilling outcome, whatever that may look like for you.

Commit to Becoming a Better You

This is the crème de la crème of building a healthy, strong relationship. While it is easy to point out the flaws in our significant other, it is equally important to recognize our own shortcomings. The best gift you can give to your spouse is the commitment to your own self-improvement. It is not your job to fix your partner but to work on bettering yourself.

When we focus on addressing our own issues, admitting our faults, and taking accountability for our actions, we set ourselves on the right path. A downward spiral in a marriage often involves both parties failing to see their own role in the problems and instead focusing solely on their partner's mistakes.

Consider this analogy: in a car accident, when one person is at fault, the insurance adjuster will investigate to determine if everyone involved did everything possible to avoid the accident. They ask the critical question, "What did you do to avoid this accident?" If they find that you could have done something differently to prevent the crash, your claim might not be honored.

Similarly, in a relationship, it is important to ask yourself what you can do to prevent your marriage from falling apart, even if some of the issues are due to your partner's actions. For every action, there is a reaction. Understanding this can be deeply explored in therapy, and I strongly suggest working with a relationship coach.

Committing to self-improvement will not only benefit your marriage but also enhance your overall quality of life. Sometimes, we don't recognize our own insecurities or behavioral issues until someone points them out. It can be painful to realize that our negative behaviors have caused pain to others but remember that hurt people hurt people. The good news is that help is available, and when we learn better, we do better.

Things you can do to help bring out the best version of yourself:

- **Work with a Relationship Coach:**Professional guidance can help you understand and address your own issues.
- **Counseling:**Therapy provides a safe space to explore personal challenges and growth.
- **Read Self-Help Books:**Gain insights and strategies for personal development.
- **Love Yourself:**Self-love is the foundation for all healthy relationships.
- **Have Personal Time:**Take time for yourself to recharge and reflect.
- **Meditate:**Practice mindfulness to reduce stress and improve mental clarity.
- **Personal Affirmations:**Use positive affirmations to build self-confidence and self-worth.
- **Pray:**For those who find solace in spirituality, prayer can be a powerful tool for personal growth.
- **Eat Healthier:**Nutrition plays a crucial role in overall well-being.
- **Rest:**Ensure you are getting enough sleep to maintain your physical and mental health.
- **Have an Attitude of Gratitude:**Focus on the positives in your life and appreciate what you have.
- **Journal:**Writing down your thoughts can help you process emotions and track personal growth.
- **Limit Activities That Deplete You:**Prioritize activities that energize you and avoid those that drain you.
- **Find What Makes You Happy:**Engage in hobbies and activities that bring you joy.

- **Be Okay with Saying No:** Set boundaries to protect your time and energy.
- **Drink Plenty of Water:** Staying hydrated is essential for overall health.

By committing to these practices, you can become the best version of yourself, contributing positively to your relationships and your life.

About the Author

Sherita is a mother of one. She has been self-employed for most of her adult life, spanning back to the age of 21 years old. Sherita has been a phenomenal hairstylist for over 30 years, servicing countless faithful clients over the course of her tenure. Later, she found her second career as a real estate agent. In 2020, when our world experienced a horrible pandemic where Covid-19 took countless lives, including many of her family members that were dear to her, Sherita founded SoSherita, an online women's clothing store. Sherita then found herself as a radio host on a local radio station for a short while. She joined in holy matrimony in 2020 during the pandemic in the backyard of her parents' home, with only a few witnesses watching from a safe distance. This is Sherita's second marriage; she was previously married for 14 years.

Throughout her life, Sherita has gained much wisdom and knowledge from her personal experiences. Through her personal experiences and observing the experiences of others, Sherita has learned how to navigate through relationships. She has learned how to fix her negative behavior and take accountability for her role in the breakdown of her past relationships, not just for herself but for the life and good health of her relationship. She has learned through much pain and disappointment how to forgive. Sherita has learned the importance of quality and effective communication between two people. It is during the rough patches in her previous marriage and current marriage and non-marital relationships that she learned the value and importance of respect, self-love, courage, forgiveness, and unselfishness.

Sherita, now 54 at the time of writing this book, is married, with nearly 40 years of relationship experience. She has a lot to share and is eager to help both young and older couples who are struggling to maintain a healthy relationship or get back on course to a marriage that has gone through their own personal fiery circumstances. So many people lose hope after so much disappointment and believe that there is no more hope for their marriage or relationship. I am here to tell you that there is hope. After all the mistakes, of which I have made many, if I can be quite transparent with you, and the ups and downs with the good, bad, and ugly, your marriage can survive the worst ordeals if both parties are willing to forgive one another. Remember this one thing: if you want to be forgiven for your mistakes and offenses you have made against other people, then you too must forgive. After all, NO one is perfect. Nevertheless, with some work, full cooperation, some faith, and a change of bad behaviors, your marriage can survive.

Message from the Author

My hope is that "Love on the Hot Seat: Marriage Rewind" has brought your relationship to a better place where you and your spouse can enjoy a happy, blissful marriage in peace and harmony. Remember that your spouse is not perfect and will make mistakes, just like you. Continue to be patient and forgiving, just as you have been forgiven. May your marriage be strengthened, made whole, and truly abide until death do you part.

To my beloved parents, Doris and Godfrey Martin,

This book is dedicated to the memory of my father, Godfrey, and the enduring strength of my mother, Doris. Their 49-year marriage was a testament to their unbreakable bond and unwavering support for each other. Together, they faced numerous challenges, from health struggles to financial difficulties, yet their resilience and love never faltered.

My father, Godfrey, a Vietnam veteran, demonstrated immense bravery and sacrifice throughout his life. His courage and steadfastness were matched by my mother's devotion as she managed the complexities of raising five children with grace and determination. Their shared journey through life's storms has been a profound lesson in endurance for me.

Though my father passed away on September 10, 2018, his legacy of strength and love continues to inspire me. My mother remains a pillar of fortitude and grace, and their combined influence has shaped who I am today.

With heartfelt gratitude and love,

Sherita

Help Line

If you or someone you know is experiencing physical abuse, it is important to seek help immediately. The National Domestic Violence Hotline in the United States is available 24/7 and provides confidential support to those affected by domestic violence.

National Domestic Violence Hotline

- **Phone:** 1-800-799-SAFE (7233)
- **Website:** https://thehotline.org
- **Text:** Text "START" to 88788

They offer support through calls, chat, and text, and can provide resources and guidance on how to stay safe, access shelters, and receive counseling and legal assistance. If you are in immediate danger, please call 911 or your local emergency services.

NEED A RELATIONSHIP COACH?
AVAILABLE FOR COUPLES & GROUP BOOKINGS

Appointments made by contacting: asksherita@yahoo.com